Teens and Body Image

Christine Wilcox

Teen Well-Being

ReferencePoint
Press®

San Diego, CA

About the Author

Christine Wilcox writes fiction and nonfiction for young adults and adults. She has worked as an editor, an instructional designer, and a writing instructor. She lives in Richmond, Virginia, with her husband, David, and her son, Doug.

© 2016 ReferencePoint Press, Inc.
Printed in the United States

For more information, contact:
ReferencePoint Press, Inc.
PO Box 27779
San Diego, CA 92198
www.ReferencePointPress.com

Picture credits:
Cover: Thinkstock Images
Depositphotos: 11, 15
Steve Zmina: 30, 31, 32, 45, 46, 47, 48, 61, 62, 63, 76, 77, 78

LIBRARY OF CONGRESS CATALOGING-IN-PUBLICATION DATA

Wilcox, Christine.
  Teens and body image / by Christine Wilcox.
    pages cm. -- (Compact research)
  Includes bibliographical references and index.
  ISBN 978-1-60152-828-5 (hardback) -- ISBN 1-60152-828-0 (hardback) 1. Body image in adolescence--Juvenile literature. 2. Body image--Juvenile literature. I. Title.
  BF724.3.B55W55   2016
  155.5'12--dc23
                                                                        2015012871

Contents

Foreword

❝Where is the knowledge we have lost in information?❞

—T.S. Eliot, "The Rock."

As modern civilization continues to evolve, its ability to create, store, distribute, and access information expands exponentially. The explosion of information from all media continues to increase at a phenomenal rate. By 2020 some experts predict the worldwide information base will double every seventy-three days. While access to diverse sources of information and perspectives is paramount to any democratic society, information alone cannot help people gain knowledge and understanding. Information must be organized and presented clearly and succinctly in order to be understood. The challenge in the digital age becomes not the creation of information, but how best to sort, organize, enhance, and present information.

ReferencePoint Press developed the *Compact Research* series with this challenge of the information age in mind. More than any other subject area today, researching current issues can yield vast, diverse, and unqualified information that can be intimidating and overwhelming for even the most advanced and motivated researcher. The *Compact Research* series offers a compact, relevant, intelligent, and conveniently organized collection of information covering a variety of current topics ranging from illegal immigration and deforestation to diseases such as anorexia and meningitis.

The series focuses on three types of information: objective single-author narratives, opinion-based primary source quotations, and facts and statistics. The clearly written objective narratives provide context and reliable background information. Primary source quotes are carefully selected and cited, exposing the reader to differing points of view, and facts and statistics sections aid the reader in evaluating perspectives. Presenting these key types of information creates a richer, more balanced learning experience.

For better understanding and convenience, the series enhances information by organizing it into narrower topics and adding design features that make it easy for a reader to identify desired content. For example, in *Compact Research: Illegal Immigration*, a chapter covering the economic impact of illegal immigration has an objective narrative explaining the various ways the economy is impacted, a balanced section of numerous primary source quotes on the topic, followed by facts and full-color illustrations to encourage evaluation of contrasting perspectives.

The ancient Roman philosopher Lucius Annaeus Seneca wrote, "It is quality rather than quantity that matters." More than just a collection of content, the *Compact Research* series is simply committed to creating, finding, organizing, and presenting the most relevant and appropriate amount of information on a current topic in a user-friendly style that invites, intrigues, and fosters understanding.

Teens and Body Image at a Glance

What Is Body Image?

Body image refers to the way individuals think and feel about their body. Body image is not dependent on the body's actual size or shape and has little to do with a person's actual appearance.

The Difference Between Positive and Negative Body Image

People with a positive body image are objective about their bodies and do not allow their bodies to affect their self-esteem. People with a negative body image cannot see their bodies objectively and equate the state of their bodies with their self-worth.

Body Criticism from Peers Impacts Body Image

Because teens are going through a myriad of physical, emotional, and social changes during adolescence, they often tease others about body changes. Most do this to feel better about themselves and their status among their peers. This type of bullying can damage self-esteem and cause negative body image.

Puberty Affects Body Image

Many of the issues that teens have with their bodies are related to the changes that take place during puberty. For this reason, differences in height, weight, muscle development in boys, and breast development in girls are often areas of concern.

Boys Also Struggle with Negative Body Image

Body image is typically thought of as a female concern. However, research has shown that many boys are also concerned about their appearance.

The Media Affects Body Image

The media tends to use actors and models who embody cultural beauty stereotypes. This can cause teens to aspire to a standard of beauty that is unattainable for all but a small percentage of the population.

Weight Bias Is Prevalent in Society

Studies have shown that weight bias—the tendency to associate negative characteristics with excess weight—can cause overweight teens to be treated poorly by their peers, their teachers, and even their families.

Social Media Causes People to Feel Worse About Their Bodies

Even though social media features pictures of everyday people, studies have shown that it makes most people feel worse about their bodies. This is because people tend to post only flattering and digitally manipulated photographs of themselves.

Negative Body Image Can Lead to Serious Mental Disorders

A small percentage of people with negative body image will go on to develop mental disorders such as depression, body dysmorphic disorder, eating disorders, or self-harm behaviors.

Talk Therapy Can Improve Body Image

Talk therapy, such as cognitive behavioral therapy, has been shown to improve body image. However, complaining about one's body to friends—also known as "fat talk"—has been shown to make body image worse.

Self-Acceptance Improves Self-Esteem

Teens who accept their bodies as they are and stop equating their body size and shape with their self-worth find that their self-esteem improves.

Overview

66You look how you look. Be comfortable. What are you going to do? Be hungry every single day to make people happy?99

—Jennifer Lawrence, an Academy Award–winning American actor.

66I was one of the only girls in my high school that didn't get a nose job. And if anybody needed it, I probably did. I'm proud . . . to be a voice for girls and say, 'You don't need to look like everybody else. Love who you are.'99

—Lea Michele, American actor and star of the TV show *Glee*.

When Haley Kilpatrick started middle school, the girls at her lunch table began to criticize the appearances of their classmates. "The *tiniest* things caught their attention, like who had wax in his ears or who didn't shave her legs," Kilpatrick writes in *The Drama Years: Real Girls Talk About Surviving Middle School*. "Since I was often a target too, I felt constantly on guard when I sat with them: When would *my* appearance be up for discussion?" Soon Kilpatrick began to feel self-conscious about her own body and was afraid to do anything that might expose it to criticism—like auditioning for the dance team or trying out for cheerleading. "I knew my fear was holding me back," she writes. "But at the time, it felt like a matter of social survival."[1]

When she got older, Kilpatrick realized that nearly all tweens and teens—both girls and boys—experience anxiety about their changing bodies. This anxiety can be heightened by negative messages from their peers and their families, as well as by unrealistic images portrayed in the media. As a result, some teens begin to dislike their own bodies and develop what experts call body dissatisfaction or negative body image.

What Is Body Image?

Body image refers to the way individuals view their body. Body image is not simply a mental picture of the body. As an aspect of self-image, body image includes the thoughts, feelings, and behaviors related to the body.

According to the National Eating Disorders Collaboration, there are four aspects to body image. One is perceptual. The perceptual aspect of body image has to do with the way people believe they look. This perception is not always accurate, especially among adolescents, whose bodies are rapidly changing. For instance, a study by Harvard University found that up to two-thirds of underweight twelve-year-old girls thought they were overweight—an example of perceptual body image not matching actual appearance.

A second aspect of body image is known as affective. This aspect of body image has to do with how people feel about the way they look. When affective body image is negative, it is sometimes referred to as body dissatisfaction.

A third aspect of body image—the cognitive aspect—involves the beliefs

> **Nearly all tweens and teens—both girls and boys—experience anxiety about their changing bodies.**

people have in regard to their body. For instance, some people believe that they will look better or feel better if they lose weight or gain muscle.

Finally, the behavioral aspect of body image encompasses the things people do in response to the thoughts and feelings about their body. Dieting and exercising are behavioral responses to negative body image, as are disordered eating and self-isolation. Experts often talk about behavioral body image when discussing features of eating disorders, such as binging and purging.

Body Image Is Not About Appearance

Body image has very little to do with actual appearance. Instead, it is usually formed in response to personal beliefs, cultural values, and the perceived attitudes of others. According to David Schlundt, a psychologist at Vanderbilt University, "All of your experiences, all the teasing you went through as a child, all the self-consciousness you had as a teenager, and all the worrying about whether you would be accepted as good enough or attractive enough are called forth" when people think about their bodies. "It's not a perceptual thing. It's a combination of emotion, meaning and experience."[2]

The concept that body image and actual appearance have little to do with each other can be hard for teenagers to grasp. Because they live in their bodies and see themselves in the mirror (or in photographs or videos) every day, teens often assume that their perceptions of their bodies are based on reality. However, the feedback teens get from their peers and families—as well as the comparisons they make to images they see in the media—have much more influence on their body image than what they actually look like. This is why it is possible for teens to have a negative body image and still be regarded as attractive by society. Conversely, many teens who may not meet society's standards of attractiveness are happy with their appearance and have a positive body image.

> " **Body image has very little to do with actual appearance.** "

Body image also changes over time—sometimes from moment to moment. For instance, studies have shown that activities like shopping for clothes or eating fattening foods can make people believe—for a short time at least—that they are fatter or more unattractive than they previously thought. Body image also tends to improve as people get older, regardless of what they look like.

Positive Versus Negative Body Image

Body image is linked to self-esteem and is part of our self-image. The Cleveland Clinic, one of the most highly rated medical centers in the United States, describes self-image as "an internal dictionary that describes the characteristics of the self, including intelligent, beautiful, ugly, talented, selfish, and kind. These characteristics form a collective representation of our assets and liabilities as we see them."[3]

Teens with a healthy self-image tend to have a positive body im-

Most teens assume that their perceptions of body image are based on what they see when they look in the mirror. Experts say that body image actually has little to do with one's appearance and more to do with personal beliefs, cultural values, and the perceived attitudes of others.

age, and vice versa. They are able to assess their bodies objectively and realistically and are not overly concerned about others' perceptions or judgments. They understand that bodies come in a variety of shapes and sizes, and they are able to appreciate their bodies as they are. According to experts at Brown University, "Healthy body image means that our assessment of our bodies is kept separate from our sense of self-esteem, and it ensures that we don't spend an unreasonable amount of time worrying about food, weight and calories." These experts say that teens with a healthy body image understand that "physical appearance says very little about our character or value as a person."[4] Such teens tend to be more confident, more social, and more willing to try new things.

Teens who have a negative or poor body image tend to allow their perceptions about how they look to affect their feelings of self-worth. They often believe that if they could only change their appearance, their problems would disappear. Because of this, teens with negative body image can spend huge amounts of time thinking about their bodies. This tendency often continues into adulthood—especially when it comes to issues about body weight. According to Brown University's Health Services Department, "In one study of college students, 74.4 percent of the normal-weight women stated that they thought about their weight or appearance 'all the time' or 'frequently.' But the women weren't alone; the study also found that 46 percent of the normal-weight men surveyed responded the same way."[5]

Unfortunately, this preoccupation tends to worsen body image, leading to a vicious circle of preoccupation and body dissatisfaction. Teens caught in this unhealthy cycle often feel self-conscious and anxious. They sometimes avoid trying new things, do poorly in school, and are more at risk for developing life-threatening illnesses like depression, obesity, and eating disorders. Bullying or teasing by others can reinforce their feelings of low self-worth, and they sometimes isolate themselves to avoid perceived—or real—criticism of their appearance.

Appearances Matter

One reason that teens become preoccupied with their appearance is that they understand that in modern society, appearances do matter. Regardless of how a society defines beauty, studies have found that attractive people tend to have advantages over less-attractive people. Attractive children are more popular with their peers and their teachers, and teachers tend to expect more of attractive children. According to psychologist Rebecca Puhl, "Educators report lower expectations for overweight students than normal weight across a variety of performance areas, and physical educators perceive overweight students to have worse social, reasoning, physical, and cooperation abilities than non-overweight students."[6] As adults, attractive people tend to earn more money, have higher social status, and are even found guilty less often in court. "We do ourselves a disservice by saying looks don't matter in society," says Connor Principe, a psychology professor at

> **Attractive people tend to have advantages over less-attractive people.**

Pacific University. "We're told it's what's on the inside that matters, and to never judge a book by its cover. That's counterproductive. We need to say, Looks do matter."[7]

Lisa Damour, director of the Laurel School's Center for Research on Girls, in Ohio, notes that the media reinforces the notion that looks matter. She points out that teens who are anxious about how they look are "coming to this anxiety in the context of a culture that cares a whole lot about appearance, very rarely puts anybody who is less than almost perfectly attractive in front of them on TV or in the media, and, on top of that, sends the message that the body is infinitely mutable and can and should be changed for the better."[8] These messages not only support the idea that more-attractive people are somehow better than less-attractive people, they reinforce the notion that being less attractive is a personal failing that reflects a person's worth.

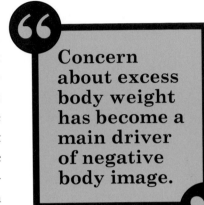

Concern about excess body weight has become a main driver of negative body image.

Excess body weight is one aspect of appearance that society usually equates with personal failure. In the media, attractive people are almost always thin and fit, and overweight people are almost always portrayed as unattractive, socially inept, lazy, stupid, or simply low on the social ladder. Teen girls are especially sensitive to these messages because they naturally put on weight during puberty. And with one-third of American children and teens overweight or obese, concern about excess body weight has become a main driver of negative body image.

Why Are Teens Especially Critical of Each Other's Bodies?

Puberty—which usually starts between age eight and thirteen in girls and nine and fifteen in boys—is the time when children typically begin to have issues with body image. This usually coincides with the middle school years (in the United States, middle school spans sixth through eighth grades). These years can be a tumultuous time for young people. According to Kilpatrick, "Middle schoolers are faced with overwhelming changes—biological, hormonal, social, emotional—in a very short period of time." These changes create what she calls "a perfect storm of self-consciousness"[9] among adolescents.

Teasing, bullying, and excluding others is one way some people respond to these feelings of insecurity. "Girls feel bad about their own body image and they need to get their anger out, so they make fun of other people,"[10] explains Tabitha, a sixth grader in New York. Other teens may tease or exclude each other in order to create a feeling of superiority and belonging. According to bullying expert Joel Haber, as much as 95 percent of all bullying has the goal of protecting or increasing the perpetrator's status within a group. And since most adolescents are already self-conscious about their changing bodies, bullies often zero in on their targets' appearance. In a 2014 survey of fifteen hundred teens aged thirteen to seventeen, 64 percent report they have been bullied about their physical appearance at least once—more than any other factor.

Some adults view being teased about appearance as a necessary rite of passage. They believe that enduring this type of bullying gives teens an opportunity to practice dealing with the types of peer conflicts they will encounter in the adult world. Kilpatrick disagrees. She believes that bullying among teens is far harsher than anything they will encounter as adults. "While there may be backstabbing and gossip at your office or workplace, or among a group of friends, when was the last time someone walked up to you and pointed out to everyone, in the cruelest way possible, the *one* flaw you've been desperately trying to hide? *That's* middle school."[11]

What Types of Issues Do Teens Have with Their Bodies?

Although some body image issues are more common than others, people can become self-conscious about any aspect of appearance—from the size of one's forehead to the shape of one's toes. In the tween and teen years, many body image issues have to do with body changes that occur during puberty. Adolescents do not all go through puberty at the same time, and girls tend to enter puberty before boys. For this reason, discrepancies in height, weight, muscle development (in boys), breast development (in girls), and the onset of secondary sexual characteristics (such as body hair) can all become areas of concern. Acne, which often accompanies puberty, often causes self-consciousness and embarrassment. Excess body weight—regardless of whether it is a normal response to puberty—also

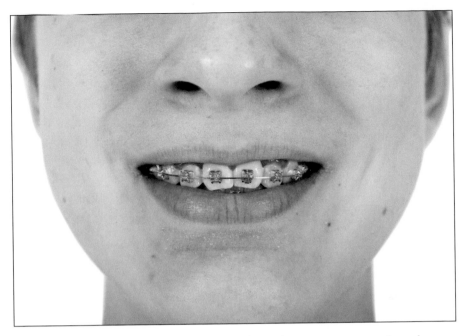

Teens sometimes become self-conscious about their appearance when they focus on one physical characteristic—for example, crooked teeth or freckles. Self-consciousness can be magnified when they compare themselves to images they see in the media.

tends to cause body dissatisfaction, especially as teens become interested in the opposite sex.

Teens can also become self-conscious about their overall attractiveness—especially when they compare themselves to the images they see in the media. Freckles, protruding ears, a prominent nose, crooked teeth, or anything else that deviates from society's definition of attractiveness can affect a teen's body image. However, in many cases body image issues that relate to overall attractiveness become less important in adulthood or disappear entirely.

What Contributes to Negative Body Image?

Teens' body images are strongly affected by the images they see in the media. Television, movies, magazines, and the Internet are all filled with examples of society's concept of beauty. Even cartoons exaggerate masculine and feminine ideals; male cartoon characters are often broad chested and muscular, and female characters have exaggerated breasts and tiny waists. Teens who have grown up with these media images often aspire to look like them—and when they cannot, their body image suffers.

Even though the media often sets the standard for attractiveness in modern culture, it actually has less of an effect on teens' body image than the influence of family, friends, and peers. Teasing and bullying can be particularly damaging to body image. The humiliation and shame that can follow a bullying attack can cause teens to become extremely self-conscious about their bodies, triggering distortions in body perception that can follow a teen into adulthood.

What Are the Consequences of Negative Body Image?

Teens who struggle with negative body image tend to spend a great deal of time thinking about their bodies. Mental health experts refer to this type of preoccupation as rumination. Rumination—or excessively worrying about a problem without being able to develop strategies to solve it—is linked to depression and anxiety, serious mental health issues that interfere with daily life. Excessive body rumination can also prevent teens from making friends, trying new things, pursuing their dreams, or simply enjoying life.

Negative body image has also been linked to several serious disorders. Body dysmorphic disorder (BDD) and eating disorders like anorexia and bulimia are all mental health disorders in which the sufferer has developed an extremely distorted view of his or her body. Teens who have BDD believe that one or more of their features—such as their nose or their chin—is extremely ugly. Teens with anorexia and bulimia view their bodies as much heavier than they actually are and go to extreme lengths to lose weight. People with BDD or eating disorders obsess about the appearance of their bodies to the extent that their distorted body image takes over their lives. Although having a poor body image does not itself cause these disorders, it can trigger them in vulnerable people.

> " Freckles, protruding ears, a prominent nose, crooked teeth, or anything else that deviates from society's definition of attractiveness can affect a teen's body image. "

How Can Teens Improve Their Body Image?

Many teens believe that in order to have a positive body image and improve their self-esteem, they must change the way their bodies appear to other people. However, studies have shown that improving negative body image actually increases the ability to make positive changes to the body. According to the Cleveland Clinic, "Learning to have a positive relationship with an imperfect body increases the ability to lose weight."[12] Improving body image is also a key part of recovery for eating disorders and other serious illnesses related to body image.

To improve body image, experts suggest a good place to start is limiting exposure to people and situations that increase body self-consciousness. Asking friends and family to stop engaging in body-shaming talk and avoiding peers who are critical of appearance can help improve body image. Therapy can be helpful as well; learning to challenge negative thoughts and stop rumination are techniques that a qualified counselor or therapist can help people learn. Educating oneself about the ways that media images promote body dissatisfaction can also help improve body image.

> "Improving body image is . . . a key part of recovery for eating disorders."

Developing a positive body image is also one of the best defenses against teasing, bullying, and social exclusion. Teens who do not equate their appearance with their self-worth are protected from the debilitating feelings of shame that can accompany body criticism from peers. For instance, when fourteen-year-old Carleigh O'Connell learned that her peers had spray painted a comment about her body on a rock at a public beach, she decided to respond with pride rather than shame. "I could have just walked away, cried in my room or tried to ignore it altogether, but that wasn't an option for me," she writes on the blog *A Mighty Girl*. Instead, she posted a picture of herself posing with the graffiti on Instagram. "I have realized that owning who you are and how you are made is much better than feeling ashamed or bad about yourself,"[13] she writes.

It Gets Better

As teens mature and enter early adulthood, many find that their body image naturally improves. With puberty-induced body changes behind them, most young adults become more comfortable in their bodies. Teens entering college or the workplace often find that as more body types are represented, people are less critical of each other's appearance, and body difference is often celebrated rather than singled out.

What Issues Do Teens Have with Their Bodies?

66 [Being compared to a fat girl] shook my world—not for days, not for months, forever. **99**

—Ronna Benjamin, who writes about teenage issues with weight and body image on the website Better After 50.

66 I've gone through stages where I hate my body so much that I won't even wear shorts and a bra in my house because if I pass a mirror, that's the end of my day. **99**

—Fiona Apple, an American singer-songwriter who suffered from an eating disorder after being raped at age twelve.

Body image first became an issue for Alyssa in the seventh grade. During an experiment in science class, she found out that she weighed as much as one of the boys. "I took that like, I should weigh less; otherwise I won't be seen as pretty," she said. Even though she was the smallest girl in her class, she went on a diet, losing so much weight that her family became concerned. "For a few months I was in denial and didn't want to admit that [losing so much weight] was unhealthy, because I liked being tiny," she explains. "But to my family, my personality was changing because I was so worried about it."[14]

Like Alyssa, many teens first became concerned with how they look in middle school, when the onset of puberty begins to change teens' bodies. These changes start at different times and progress at different rates, and boys and girls cannot help but compare their bodies to the bodies of their peers. Girls tend to be more body conscious and have more problems with negative body image than boys, but experts are finding that negative body image among boys is more of a problem than previously thought.

Girls worry about the size of their breasts and hips, and those who are tall or have a larger body type can feel uncomfortable around smaller or shorter peers—especially boys. Boys worry about being shorter or less muscular than their peers. Both boys and girls worry about being overweight. They also become concerned about their overall attractiveness—which can be affected by acne or braces. Finally, as teens become interested in the opposite sex, they become worried about the changes to their genitalia.

Puberty and Weight

Body weight is often a significant factor in body image. This is especially true for girls, who are surrounded by media images and messages that tell them that being fat is unacceptable. According to psychologists Eleanor Wertheim and Susan Paxton, "Adolescent girls often think that being thinner would make them happier, healthier, and better looking."[15]

> " Negative body image among boys is more of a problem than [experts] previously thought. "

What many teens do not realize is that weight gain during puberty is both healthy and natural. Between ages eleven and fourteen, most girls gain about 40 pounds (18 kg) as their bodies develop. Boys enter puberty one or two years later and can gain much more. Many boys and girls go through a short period when they appear overweight—their body has retained fat but they have not yet gotten taller. This can cause intense anxiety in some adolescents—worry that is sometimes echoed by their parents, their coaches, or even their doctors. However, if sudden weight gain in adolescence is not caused by a medical problem, teens should not worry. Instead, experts suggest concentrating on eating healthy foods, getting plenty of exercise, and allowing body weight to normalize on its own.

Weight and Body Image

Even though a certain amount of weight gain is a natural part of puberty, about one in five teens struggles with obesity—which in the United States is defined as having a body mass index of 30 or above. Since the 1980s (when only about one in twenty teens was obese), rates of childhood obesity have increased dramatically. The reason for the increase is not clear. However, being overweight or obese can significantly damage body image. Overweight teens can be profoundly affected by negative reactions to their appearance from peers, teachers, coaches, family members, and society in general.

Being underweight is also problematic—especially for teen boys. Boys who are leaner than their peers are subject to teasing, physical bullying, and social exclusion. "A boy who is skinny is associated with being weak or small or maybe they are teased and called a 'girl,'"[16] explains body image expert Robyn Silverman. Boys are also more likely to use dangerous methods to try to gain muscle, such as binge eating, excessive exercise, or steroid use.

> " Being over-weight or obese can significantly damage body image. "

Height and Dating

"I was in eighth grade when I started to notice that I was different from everyone else," remembers Kimberly Couzens, a blogger for the online newspaper *Huffington Post*. "I grew from 5'4" to 5'9" in a single school year and my subsequent awkwardness was obvious." Couzens, who reached a final height of five feet eleven inches, remembers how self-conscious her height made her feel. "My height was an unavoidable reminder that I was different, and being different isn't cool or fun when you're a teenager who wants to fit in."[17]

Girls who are tall or who go through an early growth spurt can feel clumsy and unfeminine—especially when they compare themselves to their thinner, lighter peers. Meanwhile, boys who are short or who get their growth spurt late can feel as though their stature makes them less masculine. Both situations can impact teen dating. Teens who are just starting to date are often extremely self-conscious, and a discrepancy in height can add to that self-consciousness. For instance, a tall girl might hesitate to date a short boy not because she finds his size unattractive but because being with him makes her self-conscious about her own height.

Studies show that taller girls tend to become more comfortable with their height as they get older. Shorter boys do as well. According to psychologist Duncan Thomson, short men "are quite capable of being content and at ease with their appearance."[18] And self-confidence and a positive body image can be attractive to the opposite sex—regardless of one's height.

Muscle Development in Boys

At one time, it was primarily boys who were concerned about muscle growth and definition. Today both girls and boys want six-pack abs, and girls and women alike admire the defined biceps of First Lady Michelle Obama. However, boys tend to equate their musculature with their masculinity. From a young age, boys view large, defined muscles as a sign of attractiveness, maturity, and social stature. According to Carolyn Savage, a former teacher and elementary school principal, "Size is so important in the social pecking order of young boys."[19] For this reason, many boys entering puberty are concerned about their muscle development—especially if their peers are already muscular.

The body shape of teen boys tends to change during their growth spurt. According to *The Merck Manual of Medical Information*, peak growth typically happens to boys between ages thirteen and fifteen—though it can happen several years later. This is the time that shoulders broaden and muscles in the chest (pectorals) and arms (biceps and triceps) begin to get bigger. After puberty, teen boys can increase muscle mass through resistance training (lifting weights). However, lifting weights before puberty will not increase muscle mass and can even cause injury. Because of this, boys who are in the early stages of puberty should not lift weights unless their doctor approves.

> " **Both girls and boys want six-pack abs.** "

Boys, Body Size, and Self-Esteem

Recently, researchers have begun to pay more attention to the way teen boys' perception of their size and musculature affects their body image and self-esteem. A 2012 study published in the journal *Pediatrics* found that more than 90 percent of middle- and high-school boys exercise at least occasionally to build muscle. In addition, two 2014 studies published in the journal *Psychology of Men and Masculinity* found that boys who were underweight were more likely to use steroids and feel depressed—especially if they only perceived themselves to be underweight. "These studies highlight the often underreported issue of distorted body image among adolescent boys," says psychologist Aaron Blashill. "We found that some of these boys who feel they are unable to achieve that often unattainable image are suffering and may be taking drastic measures."[20]

> " Only a small percentage of men have the genetic propensity to be both muscular and lean. "

That unattainable image—of a heavily muscled yet lean male—tends to be the physique currently favored by the media. However, only a small percentage of men have the genetic propensity to be both muscular and lean. Most men and older teens cannot build muscle without also gaining body fat. Others simply have bodies that are naturally lean, and they are unable to build large muscles without taking dangerous substances like steroids.

Girls, Breasts, and Body Image

Girls' breasts begin to develop in the first stages of puberty—which has been occurring earlier and earlier in recent years. Although girls still tend to get their first periods at about the same age as they did twenty years ago (between ages twelve and thirteen, on average), initial breast development can occur several years earlier than it once did. A 2010 study published in *Pediatrics* found that 10.4 percent of Caucasian, 14.9 percent of Hispanic, and 23.4 percent of African American girls had enough breast development at age seven to mark the start of puberty. No one is sure why puberty is starting so early for girls. Some believe that environmental hormones and toxins are the culprits, while others cite higher body weights. However, early breast development can have a profound effect on teen body image, because young girls are rarely able to process the attention their breasts receive—which often comes in the form of teasing or bullying.

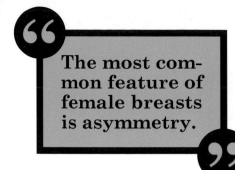

> **The most common feature of female breasts is asymmetry.**

Girls who do not develop breasts until later in adolescence also report teasing and can become equally self-conscious about their breasts, as can girls whose breasts are smaller or larger than average or who have breasts of different sizes. However, it is important to remember that normal breasts come in all shapes and sizes. In addition, the most common feature of female breasts is asymmetry. "Asymmetry is definitely the norm for women," states Dr. Michael Gartner, a plastic surgeon. "One breast is always different in shape or size than the other."[21]

Penis Size

Most experts agree that the most common cause of body anxiety among teen boys is the one they rarely discuss: penis size. During puberty, the penis grows longer. However, recent research has shown that the average penis is actually on the low side of what was previously thought to be the "normal range" of 5 to 7 inches (12.7 cm to 17.8 cm), a length that is based on data from the Kinsey Institute, which studied the issue in 1948.

A 2014 study that examined approximately fifteen thousand penis measurements taken by researchers around the world found that the average penis is actually 3.61 inches (9.2 cm) flaccid and 5.17 inches (13.1 cm) erect. This means that it is perfectly normal to have a penis that is either larger or smaller than average. In fact, researchers say that only 0.14 percent of the worldwide population has a penis that is too small to function properly. In addition, according to sex and relationship expert Ian Kerner, "The average vagina is just three to four inches deep"[22]—which means that almost every male is capable of having sexual relationships that are satisfying for both partners.

The Effect of Pornography on Girls' Body Image

Just as media images have shaped what teens consider to be the ideal body, many experts believe that online pornography has shaped their notions of "normal" genitalia. Many teens have seen online pornography—either deliberately or accidentally. Although most understand that porn stars do not have typical or average bodies, many still use porn to help them figure out how their genitalia should look.

This has sparked concern among teen girls about the appearance of their vaginas—specifically, the labia minora (the inner folds of the vagina). The labia minora often get longer during puberty, and in many women the folds protrude outside of the labia majora (the outer folds of the vagina). The labia can also be many different shapes and sizes, and they can range from light pink to deep purple or brown in color. However, women in mainstream pornography tend to have smaller, lighter-colored labia. Because many teens have only seen this type of vagina, some girls—and women— worry that their sexual partners will think that their vaginas are somehow unattractive or abnormal.

> **Many [teens] use porn to help them figure out how their genitalia should look.**

Dr. Lauren Streicher, associate professor of obstetrics and gynecology at Northwestern University's medical school, conducted a survey to see if this was true. "I ask men, 'Do you wish your partner's labia were shorter?' And, only about 2 percent have said yes," Streicher explains. "That's compared to about 30 percent of women who say they think their labia are too long. While women are obsessing about this, men are completely oblivious."[23]

Embracing Differences

It can be very difficult for teens to maintain a positive body image in the face of the dramatic changes that happen to their bodies during puberty— changes that can make them feel different from their peers. However, difference is the norm when it comes to the human body. According to students at the University of California–Santa Barbara who write the website SexInfo Online, "It is essential to remember that the human body is rarely flawless. Natural processes give us all imperfections and asymmetries, which are the details that make each individual unique. Learning to love your body in its natural form seems challenging to some people, but will ultimately bring about the most personal satisfaction."[24]

Primary Source Quotes*

What Issues Do Teens Have with Their Bodies?

❝It's a rarity to find a woman without body issues of some sort—not a full-fledged disorder, perhaps, but a skewed view of her body, a dislike of her shape, a desire to be thinner, bustier, taller, different.❞

—Zosia Mamet, "Zosia Mamet Opens Up About Her Personal Eating Disorder Struggles in *Glamour*'s September Issue," *Glamour*, September 2014. www.glamour.com.

Mamet, an actor who appears in the HBO series *Girls*, is recovering from an eating disorder.

....

❝I was always the short skinny kid. . . . Kids would jump in front of me in the line for recess and make fun of me because I was short.❞

—Quentin Vennie, "Why Men Never Discuss Body Image," *Huffington Post*, January 25, 2014. www.huffingtonpost.com.

Vennie is a certified personal trainer and health coach who helps men and women overcome negative body image.

....

* Editor's Note: While the definition of a primary source can be narrowly or broadly defined, for the purposes of Compact Research, a primary source consists of: 1) results of original research presented by an organization or researcher; 2) eyewitness accounts of events, personal experience, or work experience; 3) first-person editorials offering pundits' opinions; 4) government officials presenting political plans and/or policies; 5) representatives of organizations presenting testimony or policy.

Primary Source Quotes

26

❝ Part of me feels that if I want to be liked I have to have big breasts. ❞

—Ophélia Martin-Weber, "A 14 Year Old Girl's Thoughts on Breasts, Breastfeeding, Sex Appeal, and Society," Leaky Boob, July 10, 2014. http://theleakyboob.com.

Martin-Weber is a fourteen-year-old ballet dancer.

❝ From a young age, women aspire to Barbie-like measurements that are physiologically impossible without surgery and/or starvation. . . . It's a setup for self-hatred. ❞

—Carolyn Ross, "Why Do Women Hate Their Bodies?," *World of Psychology* (blog), Psych Central, June 2, 2012. http://psychcentral.com.

Ross specializes in treating addictions, obesity, and eating disorders.

❝ I used to have horrible acne—deep, boiling pimples— the kind that hurts so badly, I didn't want to leave my house. . . . No amount of concealer and foundation could take away . . . the embarrassment I felt, or the pain of those raging pimples. ❞

—Cameron Diaz, "Cameron Diaz: 'Call a Truce with Your Body!,'" *Seventeen*, January 9, 2014. www.seventeen.com.

Diaz is an American actress and the author of the health and fitness self-help book *The Body Book*.

❝ The skinny girls think they aren't real women if they don't have sexy curves, while the bigger girls feel like they have to hide their fat and cellulite. ❞

—Olivia, "I'm Tired of Girls Hating Their Bodies," Hello Giggles, April 8, 2014. http://hellogiggles.com.

Olivia is a college student in Nashville.

❝The pressure on boys to be 'toned and muscular' represents a return to a traditional notion of masculinity and what it means to be a man.❞

—Peggy Drexler, "Beauty and the Boy: The Impact of Negative Body Image on Our Boys," *Huffington Post*, January 12, 2013. www.huffingtonpost.com.

Drexler is a research psychologist and gender scholar.

❝Having 'The jolly green giant lives here!' scrawled across my locker stung, but it was nothing compared to the discomfort I felt in my own skin.❞

—Kimberly Couzens, "How I Learned to Love Being Tall," *Huffington Post*, July 12, 2012. www.huffingtonpost.com.

Couzens is a writer who is five feet eleven inches tall.

Facts and Illustrations

What Issues Do Teens Have with Their Bodies?

- According to *Parenting* magazine, on average, girls start their growth spurt at **10 or 11 years old**, and it lasts until they are about **15**. In boys the growth spurt starts **between 11 and 12** and continues until age **17**.

- According to the National Institute on Media and the Family, **53 percent** of **13-year-old girls** are unhappy with their bodies, a number that increases to **78 percent** by age **17**.

- A 2011 survey by *Glamour* magazine found that **61 percent** of women felt ashamed of their hips, **64 percent** felt embarrassed by their stomachs, and **72 percent** were ashamed of their thighs.

- A 2012 study by the Public Health Agency of Canada found that **50 percent** of both boys and girls in tenth grade felt that they were either too thin or too fat.

- A 2001 study in the journal *Psychology of Men and Masculinity* found that up to **25 percent** of normal-weight adolescent boys perceive themselves to be underweight.

- According to psychologist Raymond Lemberg, only **1 to 2 percent** of males have the body type depicted in male action-figure toys.

Teen Girls Are the Most Critical of Their Bodies

A study by NBC's *Today* and AOL.com surveyed over two thousand adults and two hundred teens to better understand how people feel about their bodies. Participants were asked how often they had positive and negative thoughts about their appearance. Males had more positive thoughts and fewer negative thoughts about their bodies than females overall. Teen girls had the most negative thoughts, while teen boys had the most positive thoughts.

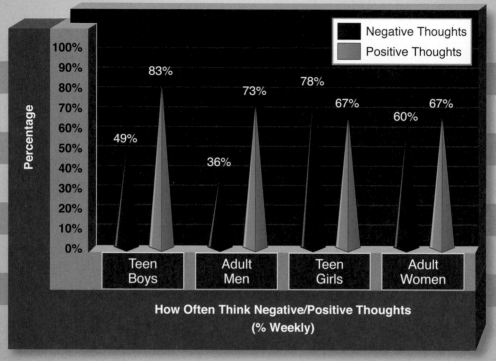

Source: *Today* and AOL.com, "Ideal to Real Body Image Survey," February 2014. www.scribd.com.

- A 2014 study in *JAMA Pediatrics* found that almost **18 percent** of teen boys are highly concerned about their physique and muscle mass.

- In 2014 researchers at Flinders University in Australia surveyed **351 women** and found that **17 percent** were interested in having labiaplasty, or plastic surgery on their vaginas.

- A 2008 study in the *Journal of Health Psychology* found that **30 percent** of men were dissatisfied with their genitals.

Teens of Both Sexes Want to Increase Muscularity

A 2012 study published in *Pediatrics* found that muscle-enhancing behaviors were more common in teen boys and girls than previously thought. The study surveyed 2,793 teens about five muscle-enhancing behaviors. While most behaviors were more common among boys, the authors concluded that muscle-enhancing behaviors among girls were significant, too. More than 40 percent of boys and 27 percent of girls said they exercised often with the aim of increasing muscle mass. In addition, almost 12 percent of boys and 6.2 percent of girls said they had used three or more behaviors in the past year.

Question: How Often Have You Employed the Following Behaviors During the Past Year?

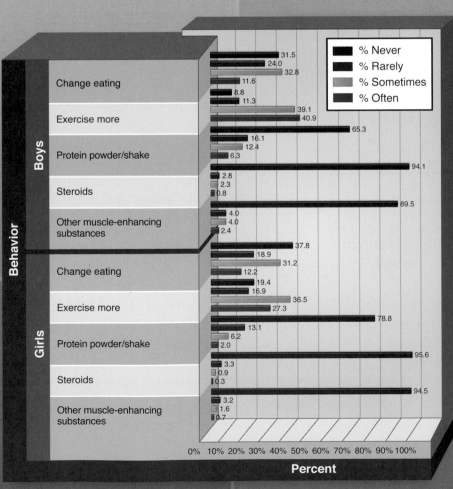

Source: Marla Eisenberg et al., "Muscle-Enhancing Behaviors Among Adolescent Girls and Boys," *Pediatrics*, December 2012. http://pediatrics.aapublications.org.

Most Teen Girls Would Change Something About Their Bodies

For a class project, two ninth-grade girls from an Australian high school surveyed their female peers about body image. Their survey found that 51 percent of the one hundred girls who participated said they were unhappy with their bodies. Eighty-one percent said they would change one or more aspects about their bodies if they could. Stomachs were the most common area of dissatisfaction, followed by legs.

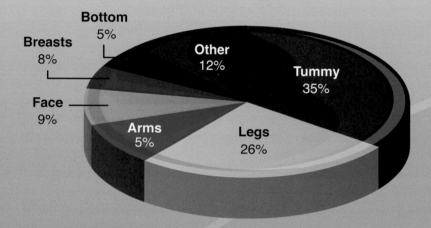

Source: Sera Tarpis and Zoe Argent, "Body Image in Teen Girls," [PowerPoint Presentation], Australian Mathematics Trust, April 19, 2013. www.featbooks.com.

- The University of California–Davis Health System estimates that **85 percent** of teens develop acne.

- According to the *Dermatology Online Journal*, up to **5.6 percent** of the population (**1 in 20 people**) is born with at least one extra, or supernumerary, nipple, which is often mistaken for a mole.

- According to Dr. Glenn Braunstein of Cedars-Sinai Medical Center, up to **two-thirds of males** will develop gynecomastia during puberty—a condition in which one or both breasts become slightly enlarged. This effect typically disappears within a year.

What Contributes to Negative Body Image?

66Our society *does* reward beauty on the outside over health on the inside.99

—Naomi Wolf, a noted feminist and author of *The Beauty Myth*.

66Even the models we see in magazines wish they could look like their own images.99

—Cheri Erdman, a therapist and author who speaks out against digitally altered images and promotes size acceptance and self-esteem.

"**B**ody image doesn't just happen," explains Caroline Knorr, the parenting editor of Common Sense Media. "It's a complex phenomenon influenced by many factors, including parents, peers, and social contexts."[25] It is also heavily influenced by the media— TV shows, movies, magazines, advertisements, and images on the Internet. Teasing and bullying also affect body image—especially when they occur in the home. When taken together, all of these influences send a powerful message that ties appearance to social status, personal happiness, and self-worth.

Media Images and Perfection

The influence on teen body image that gets talked about the most is the media. Society as a whole has a concept of physical beauty that is rarely found in the general population but is extremely common among actors and models. Males are presented as tall, lean, muscular, and handsome, and females are depicted as thin and fit, with slim hips and full breasts. These ideal body types are naturally found in about 5 percent of the population, and the actors, models, and celebrities who embody these ideals have teams of people who perfect their images—including computer graphics specialists who can digitally enhance their pictures using programs such as Photoshop. In most cases the result is that teens portrayed in movies and on TV are perfect—which gives other teens the impression that perfection is common, normal, and achievable. "The more an individual is exposed to the media, the more he or she believes it is reflective of the real world,"[26] explains eating-disorder specialist Dr. Carolyn Ross.

> " Teens portrayed in movies and on TV are perfect—which gives other teens the impression that perfection is common, normal, and achievable. "

Teens who are even slightly insecure about their changing bodies will often try to look like these perfect teens and young adults—even when they understand that the images are unrealistic. Haley Kilpatrick, who hosts a website called Girl Talk, says that the girls she talks to "all know that they're looking at falsified images and impossible-to-achieve standards, but they still see that even with the caveat of Photoshop, models are pretty—and being pretty is still the ideal."[27]

Sexualization and the Media

One of the most damaging effects of the media on body image is sexualization—specifically, the sexualization of female children and teens. The term *sexualization* refers to the way the media tends to use sexual attractiveness as a measure of worth. When the media sexualizes teens, it links traits like popularity, likability, and even morality with sexual attractiveness. "Girls get the message very early on that they must be hot and sexy in addition to being flawlessly beautiful and impossibly thin,"[28] explains Jean Kilbourne, an expert on body image and the media. These sexual stereotypes are used as a sort of shorthand to quickly sum up a character or type. For instance, in many teen-centric movies and TV shows, the lead characters tend to be well past puberty, have adult physiques, and dress to attract the opposite sex. In contrast, teen "outcast" characters tend to be unattractive, prepubescent, and conservatively dressed.

Although the media tend to sexualize girls more often than boys, studies have shown that boys are still affected by the sexualized images they encounter. In a 2013 Canadian study of both male and female high school students, the boys in the study said that sexualized images of other boys made them feel inadequate. One male participant stated that boys "see that figure on TV of being toned and muscular and whatever, and they want to be like that . . . then they can do anything from working out and getting toned . . . [or] popping drugs to make themselves bigger."[29]

When teens are constantly exposed to sexualized media images, some begin to internalize the message that one's worth should be measured by one's sexual desirability. According to the Sex Information and Education Council of Canada, this causes teens to "come to view themselves as objects to be admired and used by others, rather than as individuals with unique interests, abilities and drives."[30]

> " **Teens who self-objectify tend to see themselves from the perspective of other people.** "

Psychologists call this process self-objectification. Teens who self-objectify tend to see themselves from the perspective of other people. They constantly check their appearance and are overly concerned by how others view them. Although many teens—and adults—self-objectify to some extent, research has found that chronic self-objectification can lead to low self-esteem and body shame. In vulnerable individuals, self-objectification may also lead to depression, sexual dysfunction, and eating disorders.

Breasts, Body Image, and the Media

When Tiffany was fifteen, her breasts grew from between a B and C cup to a DD cup. For the next four years, she wore a minimizer bra and felt ashamed of her "sagging breasts, stretch marks, and down turned nipples." As she explained on her blog, *The Feminist Fist,* "All the sitcoms told me that women weren't supposed to worry about things 'not perking up' anymore until they were middle-aged or older."[31] It was also clear to Tiffany that women's large breasts tend to define them—they are either hypersexualized or objectified by men. In her view, "normal" women are small chested—but not too small, lest their lack of breasts become their defining characteristic.

The media teaches girls that the size and shape of their breasts is extremely important. Rarely is a woman shown topless unless her breasts are perfect, and cleavage is digitally added to photographs of small-chested models and celebrities. The result is that many girls become extremely self-conscious about their breasts—to the extent that they undergo plastic surgery.

> "The media teaches girls that the size and shape of their breasts is extremely important."

For Kelly, the size and shape of her breasts ruined her self-esteem and prevented her from living a happy life. Kelly had a condition called tuberous breasts (sometimes referred to as "snoopy breasts")—a congenital deformity in which there is a lack of breast tissue under the nipples. As a young adult, she "felt undeserving of love or happiness. . . . I kept my bra on during sex, and the few times a guy managed to coax it off, I felt so humiliated, I wanted to die,"[32] she admits in her essay "My Breasts Almost Ruined My Life." Eventually, Kelly—and Tiffany—had plastic surgery. However, it is possible that this step might not have been necessary if their breasts had been represented—and respected—in the media.

Weight Bias

Even though many of the bodies portrayed in the media are highly idealized, the media's choice of what to portray reflects society's values and preferences. This is never more apparent than when it comes to excess body fat.

Even though two-thirds of adults and one-third of children are overweight or obese in the United States, overweight people are almost never portrayed in the media in a positive light. Popular entertainment is filled with examples of overweight teens being mocked, pitied, bullied, or simply ignored. These teens are portrayed as being weak minded, emotionally unstable, lazy, gluttonous, or generally unlikable. For this reason, becoming overweight is a huge worry for many adolescents.

One reason that teens fear gaining weight is that they know overweight people experience weight bias—the tendency to equate a person's weight with negative characteristics and treat them accordingly. For instance, according to psychologist Rebecca Puhl, about 33 percent of overweight girls and 25 percent of overweight boys are bullied or ostracized by their classmates. In boys and girls who have the highest levels of obesity, 60 percent report being victimized by their peers.

Teens are not the only ones who judge other teens by their weight; teachers tend to have reduced expectations of students who are overweight. One survey revealed that "some teachers believed that obese persons are untidy, more emotional, less likely to succeed at work and more likely to have family problems,"[33] according to Puhl. Parents and family members can also be a source of weight bias. Puhl reports that one study found that 47 percent of overweight girls and 34 percent of overweight boys reported being teased about their weight by family members.

> " Overweight people are almost never portrayed in the media in a positive light. "

It can be extremely difficult for overweight teens to maintain a positive body image in the face of weight bias. "Consequences of weight bias can substantially reduce a child's quality of life,"[34] Puhl writes. Teens who are victimized because of their weight are vulnerable to depression, anxiety, and low self-esteem. They are also three times more likely to contemplate or try suicide than overweight teens who are not victimized.

Teasing and Bullying

Though overweight teens often face bullying, teens are teased and bullied about far more than weight issues. According to bullying expert Dr. Joel Haber, teens who are ethnic minorities, are gay or lesbian or do not conform to gender stereotypes, have social or educational difficulties, are loners, and are gifted are all at risk of being bullied. Haber says that bullies target the things that make others different—especially highly visible things such as the body. They often do so to feel better about their own bodies and to improve their social standing. According to Haber, as many as 95 percent of all bullies are trying to protect or improve their reputations in their social groups.

Bullying can have a devastating effect on body image and mental health. In response to an article about body image and bullying, one teen girl who identifies herself as "A" writes:

> Everyday, they told me how fat and ugly I was. . . . I got to a point when I was so sick from this, like physically sick. My body just manifested everything that was happening to it on the outside, and I was sick all the time. . . . I also struggle with what I think is becoming a full-fledged eating disorder because of all this bullying and because of how [bad] I feel all of the time because of what I've been told about my body and myself for so long.[35]

As A's letter shows, being bullied about one's body not only causes negative body image, it can be physically harmful. Stress-induced illness and eating disorders can be life threatening, and the mental anguish this type of bullying causes can follow a person well into adulthood.

The Opinions of Friends

One reason that teasing and bullying can be so damaging to body image is that in adolescence, peers tend to have more influence over a teen's likes, dislikes, and self-esteem than parents. Friendships are extremely important to teens—both for social support and as a way to identify oneself within the larger peer group.

Because of this, friends tend to adopt each other's beliefs and opinions. "Girls who are part of a particular friendship group have similar levels of body image concern and dietary restraint,"[36] explains psychologist Marika Tiggemann. She says that friends usually have the same opinions about what is considered normal and desirable when

> " Being bullied about one's body not only causes negative body image, it can be physically harmful. "

it comes to bodies. Fat talk—when girls and women shame themselves about their appearance as a way to bond with others—is also learned and practiced in peer groups, as are many dieting techniques. Finally, the belief that popularity is dependent on being thin or muscular is reinforced within friendship groups, and comments from friends about weight and appearance have a huge influence on a teen's body image.

Social Media

Facebook, Instagram, Tumblr, Twitter, and dozens of other social media sites are one of the main arenas in which today's teens interact with their peers. Because of this, social media can have a profound effect on body image. Teens often use social media to craft their public image, posting carefully staged photographs that have been edited with computer graphic applications so that they are as flattering as possible. These images get voted on, or liked, by their peers, and the response to any given image often influences a teen's body image and self-esteem.

> **Many experts worry that social media encourages teens to compare themselves to others.**

Many experts worry that social media encourages teens to compare themselves to others and to constantly evaluate how other people might judge their appearance. "Validation coming from [posting selfies on] social media is temporary and fickle," warns psychologist Jill Weber. "What happens when no 'likes' are provided . . . (which occurs quite regularly for teenage girls who post selfies). . . ? For girls and women with a shaky sense of identity, self-esteem plummets."[37]

However, some experts disagree. They believe that social media has a much more positive influence on body image than traditional media. According to Sarah Gervais, director of the Power and Subtle Prejudice Lab at the University of Nebraska–Lincoln, "Rather than being bombarded with [perfect images] . . . in popular magazines, television, and web pages that feed our discontent, we can look through our Instagram feed and see images of real people—with beautiful diversity. Bodies of different shapes and sizes, with diverse skin tones and complexions, without smiles always plastered to their faces."[38]

Understanding Causes Can Prevent Serious Consequences

There are many other causes of negative body image. Teens who have experienced trauma that impacts their self-esteem may struggle with their body image, and teens who suffer from certain mental illnesses may be more likely to be self-critical. Regardless of the cause, teens who are aware of the factors that influence their perceptions of their bodies have a better chance of avoiding the often serious consequences of negative body image.

Primary Source Quotes*

What Contributes to Negative Body Image?

> **"** [Posting selfies online] can be a positive exercise for your body image. . . . [It is] an opportunity to define yourself instead of having other people define you.**"**

—Laci Green, *The Selfie Revolution*, video, YouTube, December 12, 2013.
www.youtube.com/watch?v=usixSGc7T9o.

Green is a video blogger and activist who speaks about sex, body image, and feminism.

> **"** Examples of negative teen body image are all over the Web. . . . [Teens] bare themselves and beg for feedback. . . . They edit their selfies and drink in advice about how to improve their online image.**"**

—Caroline Knorr, "Is Social Media's 'Camera-Ready' Pressure Bad for Teen Body Image?," *Today*, April 30, 2014.
www.today.com.

Knorr is the parenting editor of Common Sense Media, an organization that reviews media for age appropriateness.

Bracketed quotes indicate conflicting positions.

* Editor's Note: While the definition of a primary source can be narrowly or broadly defined, for the purposes of Compact Research, a primary source consists of: 1) results of original research presented by an organization or researcher; 2) eyewitness accounts of events, personal experience, or work experience; 3) first-person editorials offering pundits' opinions; 4) government officials presenting political plans and/or policies; 5) representatives of organizations presenting testimony or policy.

❝The more time a woman spends on social media, the worse she feels about her body.❞

—Cindi Leive, *Editor: 54 Percent of Women Don't Feel Good About Bodies*, video, *Today*, October 21, 2014. www.today.com.

Leive is editor in chief of *Glamour* magazine, which conducted a survey on body image and social media.

❝Social media has the opportunity to challenge the perfect images that attack our psyche each day.❞

—Sarah Gervais, "Does Instagram Promote Positive Body Image?," *Power and Prejudice* (blog), *Psychology Today*, January 22, 2013. www.psychologytoday.com.

Gervais is an assistant professor in social and law psychology and the director of the Power and Subtle Prejudice Lab at the University of Nebraska–Lincoln.

❝Adolescent girls exist in 'an appearance culture' where media ideals and peer conversations about appearance-related topics reinforce each other.❞

—Marika Tiggemann, "Sociocultural Perspectives on Human Appearance and Body Image," in *Body Image: A Handbook of Science, Practice, and Prevention*, edited by Thomas Cash and Linda Smolak. New York: Guilford, 2012, p. 16.

Tiggemann is a professor of psychology at Flinders University in South Australia.

❝I grew up reading . . . all of the [teen fashion] magazines, not knowing anything about Photoshop. . . . I was convinced that there were these beautiful, perfect people out there, and I just wasn't one of them.❞

—Montgomery Jones, *Truth in Advertising: Should Photoshop Use Be Regulated?*, video, Representation Project, April 17, 2014. www.youtube.com/watch?v=DohcLLl7MRE.

Jones is an activist for the SPARK movement, an organization that opposes the sexualization of girls and women by the media. She attends college at Eastern Michigan University.

❝Bullying damages self-esteem and destroys body image, both which can make an individual—child or adult—susceptible to developing an eating disorder.❞

—Crystal Karges, "Being Bullied Can Lead to an Eating Disorder," Eating Disorder Hope, October 25, 2013. www.eatingdisorderhope.com.

Karges is a registered dietitian-nutritionist who writes about eating disorders.

❝The distorted, enhanced imagery [in Internet pornography] burdens teenage girls with unrealistic expectations about beauty and body image and with damaging ideas about what is attractive and sexually appealing to others.❞

—Vivian Diller, "Internet Porn and Body Image," *Face It* (blog), *Psychology Today*, September 4, 2012. www.psychologytoday.com.

Diller is a psychologist and author of *Face It: What Women Really Feel as Their Looks Change.*

Facts and Illustrations

What Contributes to Negative Body Image?

- According to eating-disorder specialist Dr. Carolyn Ross, each year teens receive about **5,260 attractiveness messages** (examples of what is or is not attractive) from network TV commercials alone.

- According to a 2014 study commissioned by the Geena Davis Institute on Gender in Media, between 2007 and 2012 the number of teen females who were at least partially nude on screen increased by **32.5 percent**.

- The Annenberg School for Communication and Journalism found that females are almost **4 times** as likely as males to be depicted in the media dressed in sexy attire.

- The National Association of Anorexia Nervosa and Associated Disorders notes that only **5 percent** of American females possess the same body type as the typical magazine model.

- According to Rader Programs, a treatment center for eating disorders, **7 out of 10 women** feel angrier and more depressed after they see fashion model images.

- Rader Programs also states that the average fashion model weighed **8 percent** less than the average woman **20 years ago**. Today the average model weighs **23 percent** less.

Teen Bullies Target Physical Appearance

Almost one quarter of Minnesota teenagers report being bullied because of their physical appearance. Twenty-three percent of all students in grades eight through eleven report being bullied about their appearance at lease once in the thirty days before the survey. Physical appearance was the most common topic of bullying, surpassing race (9 percent), sexual orientation (7 percent), gender (6 percent), and disability (5 percent). Eighth-grade girls were bullied the most about physical appearance. Studies have shown that teasing and bullying about physical appearance is linked with negative body image in the victims.

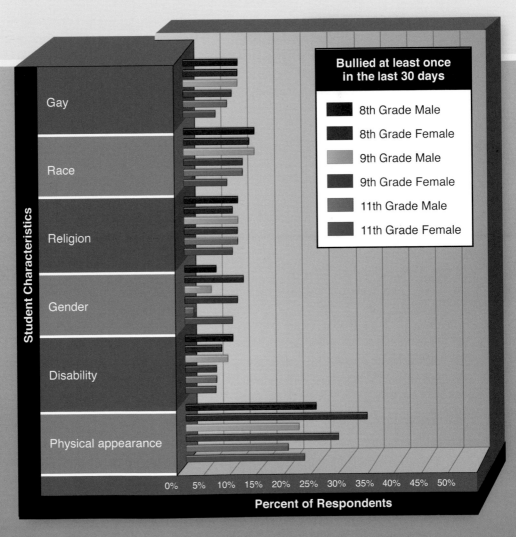

Source: Andy Birkey, "Bullying in Minnesota: A Look at the Data," *The Colu.mn,* January 28, 2014. http://thecolu.mn.

Magazine Images Cause Body Dissatisfaction in Girls

Images of models in magazines influence many girls' ideas about perfect body shape. This was the finding in a study by Rader Programs, an eating-disorder treatment center. The study, which surveyed fifth- through twelfth-grade girls, also found that these pictures often affect how they view their own bodies. Many expressed dissatisfaction with their weight even though few were actually overweight.

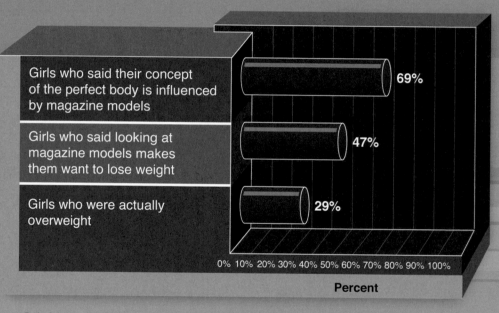

Girls who said their concept of the perfect body is influenced by magazine models	69%
Girls who said looking at magazine models makes them want to lose weight	47%
Girls who were actually overweight	29%

0% 10% 20% 30% 40% 50% 60% 70% 80% 90% 100%

Percent

Source: Rader Programs, "Women Are Dying to Be Thin," 2015. www.raderprograms.com.

- Common Sense Media reports that **87 percent** of female characters **aged 10 to 17** on the most popular children's TV shows are below average in weight.

- **Eighty-four percent** of teens and young adults who responded to a 2012 online survey conducted by the National Eating Disorders Association felt that social media has a negative effect on body image.

- A 2014 study published in *Information, Communication & Society* found that the top reason for being bullied is physical appearance.

Teen Girls Sexualized in Films

According to a 2014 study commissioned by the Geena Davis Institute on Gender in Media, teenaged girls are just as likely to be sexualized in films as young adult women. The authors analyzed roles in 120 films released globally between January 1, 2010, and May 1, 2013. They found that, among female characters, teenaged girls aged thirteen to twenty were slightly more likely to be shown in sexy attire with exposed skin than females aged twenty-one to thirty-nine. Teens were also more likely to be depicted as thin and beautiful. The study's authors note that exposure to sexualized female characters in the media can contribute to feelings of body shame.

Depiction in Films	Teens	Adults
% in sexy attire	35.6%	32.4%
% with exposed skin	33.3%	31.7%
% beautiful	20.1%	16.8%
% depicted thin	55%	49.9%

Source: Stacy Smith et al., *Gender Bias Without Borders: An Investigation of Female Characters in Popular Films Across 11 Countries.* Geena Davis Institute on Gender in Media, 2014. http://seejane.org.

- **Sixty-four percent** of teens **aged 13 to 17** report they have been bullied about their physical appearance at least once, according to a 2014 survey of **1,500 teens**.

- A study of **27 ninth graders** published in *Body Image* in 2014 found that girls who were victims of appearance-related cyberbullying most often received comments about being fat, whereas boys most often received comments about not being muscular enough.

- In a 2013 survey sponsored by Special K cereal, **93 percent** of women admitted to engaging in fat talk; **63 percent** said they do it once a week, **62 percent** said they felt compelled to do it when they hear other women doing it, and **70 percent** said they mostly talk about themselves.

Idolizing Barbie May Contribute to Eating Disorders

The popular fashion doll Barbie, created by Mattel, Inc. in 1959, may cause young girls to aspire to impossible body standards. The online organization Rehabs.com extrapolated Barbie's proportions to see whether they would be possible on a human woman. They found that Barbie's proportions are nowhere near the proportions of the average American woman. A real woman shaped like Barbie could not survive: her torso would not have enough room for her organs, and her limbs would be too thin to support her body. Eating-disorder experts believe that encouraging girls to idolize characters with unrealistic body proportions can contribute to negative body image and, in vulnerable individuals, lead to eating disorders.

Barbie vs. Real Women

Body Part	Barbie	US Average
Head	22"	21–22"
Neck	9"	12–13"
Bust	32"	35–36"
Biceps	7"	10–11"
Forearms	6"	9–10"
Wrist	3.5"	6–7"
Waist	16"	24–32"
Hips	29"	37–38"
Thigh	16"	21–22"
Calf	11"	14–15"
Ankle	6"	8–9"

Source: Sasha Goldstein, "Barbie as a Real Woman Is Anatomically Impossible and Would Have to Walk on All Fours, Chart Shows," *New York Daily News*, April 14, 2013. www.nydailynews.com.

- Nearly **50 percent** of the women in the Special K survey said that they criticized their own bodies as a way of preventing others from criticizing them.

What Are the Consequences of Negative Body Image?

66 **Girls developed eating disorders when our culture developed a standard of beauty that they couldn't obtain by being healthy. When unnatural thinness became attractive, girls did unnatural things to be thin.** 99

—Mary Pipher, a psychotherapist and the author of *Reviving Ophelia*, which examines the effects of societal pressures on adolescent girls.

66 **I looked in the mirror and I just saw someone really disgusting. A very ugly girl.** 99

—Elizabeth Delaney, who suffers from BDD, which she first developed in early adolescence.

When eighteen-year-old Ashley was in elementary school, she dreamed of playing basketball. But when she got to middle school, she was too self-conscious about her appearance to try out for the team. "I was thinking, 'I can't do this because I don't look the part,'" she remembers. "That's something I could've been good at if I'd tried. I definitely wish I'd done it. I had potential."[39]

Missing out on opportunities is just one of the ways that negative body image can impact a teen's life. Poor body image can destroy self-esteem, which can cause teens to do poorly in school and withdraw from relationships. In people who have certain vulnerabilities, negative body image can lead to dangerous mental disorders such as depression, BDD, eating disorders, and self-harming behaviors.

Quality of Life

One of the most common consequences of negative body image is increased self-consciousness. Although almost all teens feel self-conscious about their bodies at least once in a while, teens who are constantly worrying about how others perceive them cannot experience the world around them. As Alex, a thirteen-year-old girl from Washington State, says, "Sometimes when I'm out with people I get so insecure—I should've worn these jeans or this shirt. I wish I could go home and change, or just not even be there." Teens who feel this way are never fully present, and therefore miss out on important experiences. "You're not really enjoying what you're doing because you're worried about the way you look,"[40] Alex explains.

> Teens who are constantly worrying about how others perceive them cannot experience the world around them.

Teens like Alex are in danger of developing low self-esteem, which causes people to avoid situations in which they might be singled out, embarrassed, or teased. Unfortunately, being afraid of being teased can prevent teens from trying new things or exploring their interests—an important part of adolescence. As thirteen-year-old Bridget remembers, "I love music and I wanted to try out for the chorus, but that same day I had a bad hair day, and everyone was making fun of me. So I didn't go to chorus tryouts. I didn't want to make the teasing worse."[41]

When Dieting Becomes Disordered Eating

Teens who are dissatisfied with their bodies often use dieting as a way to lose weight or change their shape. Dieting can be unhealthy for teens because they need extra nutrients to fuel growth and development. When dieting is taken to an extreme, a teen is at risk of developing disordered eating.

Disordered eating refers to having an unhealthy relationship with food and body size. The difference between dieting and disordered eating lies in the way the dieter feels about food and his or her body. People who struggle with disordered eating can become obsessed with following a diet to the letter. They can be anxious about food and about being exposed to food, and they may refuse to eat in restaurants. Eating patterns and exercise routines become rigid and inflexible, and a lot of time is spent thinking about food, planning meals, and monitoring the body. Food restriction can result in a cycle of binging and purging through self-induced vomiting, excessive exercise, or laxative use. Finally, self-worth becomes completely dependent on body image or weight gain or loss, so much so that even a small weight gain can cause intense anxiety.

Psychologist Carrie Gottlieb says that disordered eating is extremely common in modern society. "In our culture there is an obsession with size and weight, diet and exercise—the pervasiveness of disordered eating is astounding. Research suggests that up to 50 percent of the population demonstrate problematic or disordered relationships with food, body, and exercise."[42]

What Are Eating Disorders?

Eating disorders are mental illnesses in which sufferers develop such intense emotions about food and body size that their thoughts and behaviors are out of their control. They often have profound disturbances in their body image, believing themselves to be much larger or smaller than they actually are. There are four types of eating disorders listed in the fifth and most recent edition of the *Diagnostic and Statistical Manual of Mental Disorders*—the guide that mental health professionals use to diagnose mental illnesses. They are anorexia nervosa, bulimia nervosa, binge eating disorder, and eating disorder not otherwise specified (EDNOS).

People with anorexia nervosa drastically restrict their food intake to lose weight and often believe they are much larger than they are. They can develop a phobia about food and be unable to eat, even when they

> The difference between dieting and disordered eating lies in the way the dieter feels about food and his or her body.

want to. People with bulimia nervosa also have body image distortions. They cycle between eating excessive amounts of food (binging) and then ridding themselves of the food through self-induced vomiting, excessive exercise, or laxative use (all referred to as purging).

People with binge eating disorder eat excessive amounts of food to deal with difficult emotions or because they erroneously believe they are underweight and need to "bulk up." Finally, people who are diagnosed with EDNOS exhibit a range of eating-disorder symptoms, but their behaviors do not fit neatly into one of the other diagnoses. Athletes who compete in sports that depend on size or weight, such as wrestlers or gymnasts, sometimes develop EDNOS. Most experts estimate that between 1 and 2 percent of the population suffer from at least one of these four eating disorders, though they acknowledge that the number may be much higher.

> **Eating disorders . . . are not dependent on a person's size or weight.**

Because eating disorders are mental illnesses and not physical ones, they are not dependent on a person's size or weight. Unfortunately, many doctors are not trained to recognize eating disorders and do not intervene unless a teen is significantly under- or overweight. This was the experience of nineteen-year-old Jasmine, who was recovering from anorexia but felt her symptoms returning. "I was struggling," she said, "but I was too worried to talk to people about it because I felt like they'd think I was overreacting because I wasn't underweight." Even her family doctor told her she had nothing to worry about because she "looked fine."[43]

According to the National Association of Anorexia Nervosa and Associated Disorders, eating disorders have the highest mortality rate of any mental disorder. However, only about one in ten sufferers seeks treatment, and only about 35 percent of them get treatment in a specialized facility. Because so many sufferers are not treated, researchers are not sure how many deaths are related to eating disorders. However, the Palo Alto Medical Foundation estimates that 20 percent of people suffering from anorexia will die prematurely from related complications such as organ damage, starvation, or suicide.

When Disordered Eating Becomes an Eating Disorder

Many of the symptoms of disordered eating and eating disorders are the same; the difference between the two is usually a matter of degree. "An individual with disordered eating is often engaged in some of the same behavior as those with eating disorders, but at a lesser frequency or lower level of severity,"[44] says Gottlieb.

Because it can be hard to know when disordered eating becomes an eating disorder, teens often report that their eating disorder took them by surprise. According to eating-disorder therapist Josie Tuttle, "It can be really hard for someone in danger of developing an eating disorder to recognize the slippery slope of the diet they're on until they're well on their way down."[45] However, only a small percentage of people with disordered eating goes on to develop eating disorders.

Eating Disorders Among Boys

Most experts say that only about one in ten people who have an eating disorder is male. However, new studies have shown that in the past fifteen years, eating disorders among males have been increasing. According to the National Association of Anorexia Nervosa and Associated Disorders, about 50 percent of people with binge eating disorder are male.

As psychologists Linda Smolak and J. Kevin Thompson explain, "If the boys who worry about being too fat are combined with the boys who worry about not being muscular enough, the percentage of adolescent boys who are body dissatisfied is often comparable to the percentage of dissatisfied girls."[46] Because body dissatisfaction, disordered eating, and eating disorders are linked, some experts think that as many as one in four people who have an eating disorder may be male.

> " **Eating disorders have the highest mortality rate of any mental disorder.** "

Body Dysmorphic Disorder

Teenager Elizabeth Delaney had always been overly concerned about her appearance. But in her last year of high school, an offhand comment about some hair growth on her face triggered an obsession with facial hair. She began to spend hours in front of the mirror, tweezing, bleaching, and waxing tiny hairs that were only visible to her. By the time she started college, her obsession with her appearance was taking over her life. It was not until she began doing research online that she was able to put a name to her obsession: body dysmorphic disorder.

BDD is a mental disorder that affects perceptual body image—how people visualize their own bodies or what they see when they look in the mirror. To people with BDD, one or more aspects of their appearance (usually a feature of their face or head) appears ugly or deformed. They become obsessed with fixing or hiding this deformity, compulsively checking the mirror, grooming themselves, and asking others how they look. As psychiatrist Katharine Phillips explains, "At least an hour a day, and on average from three to eight hours a day, they're obsessing, [saying to themselves] 'I don't look right, I look ugly.'"[47]

The obsessive nature of BDD is similar to obsessive-compulsive disorder (OCD), with a key difference. Whereas many OCD patients understand their disorder, most BDD patients do not believe they are mentally ill. "Most people with BDD are . . . certain that they really do look ugly, or deformed, or flawed in some major way,"[48] Phillips explains. Since they have such poor insight into their disorder, they rarely seek treatment. According to psychologist Ben Buchanan, "Because they think that there's actually a physical defect about them, they're not likely to visit a psychologist. They're likely to visit plastic surgeons."[49] In fact, experts believe that one-fourth of all people who seek out plastic surgery suffers from BDD.

> " To people with BDD, one or more aspects of their appearance . . . appears ugly or deformed. "

About 2.4 percent of the population has BDD. The disorder usually starts in adolescence—a time when teens develop their identities and their sense of confidence about their place in the world. However, BDD disrupts this process, destroying self-esteem and causing intense shame and self-loathing. Sufferers are highly sensitive to criticism about their appearance and report higher levels of teasing and bullying. Finally, BDD also can significantly interfere with daily life. According to the Body Dysmorphic Disorder Program at Rhode Island Hospital, "BDD in children and adolescents typically causes problems . . . [such as] poor grades, dropping out of school, withdrawing from family and friends, becoming housebound and even attempting suicide."[50]

Muscle Dysmorphia

Muscle dysmorphia (MDM) is a type of BDD in which the sufferers are obsessed with increasing their muscle mass. According to the International OCD Foundation, MDM is characterized by "being preoccupied by worries that one's body is 'too small' or 'not muscular enough' despite having a normal build, or in many cases, an objectively extremely 'buff' physique."[51]

People with MDM constantly check their appearance and compare their bodies to others'. They engage in strict diet and exercise rituals, often exercising to the point of injury. They have low self-esteem and judge their self-worth on their muscle build, and they often use supplements and steroids to increase their muscle mass. According to psychologist Lauren Muhlheim, from 50 to 100 percent of men with MDM abuse steroids—substances that promote muscle growth but that can cause emotional instability, acne, high blood pressure, and organ damage.

MDM is primarily seen among males. The prevalence of MDM is still unknown, but a 2014 study of 440 college freshmen found that 5.9 percent of them had MDM, and 75 percent of those with MDM were male. Many experts are concerned that the male stereotype that the media promotes—extremely muscular males who also have low body fat (a combination as rare as the female fashion model physique)—is skewing their perception about what is normal. "We're presenting men in a way that is unnatural," says psychologist Raymond Lemberg, who says that the new male ideal body type is even showing up in action figures. "Only 1 or 2 percent of [males] actually have that body type."[52] Also, because being strong and muscular is seen as a positive attribute, it is less likely that coaches, teachers, or parents will recognize the symptoms of MDM.

Self-Harm

Another consequence of negative body image can be self-harm, which is sometimes referred to as self-injury or cutting. Self-harm is the practice of purposely injuring oneself to reduce negative feelings. People who cut are usually not attempting suicide; instead, they are trying to relieve intense stress and release endorphins—brain chemicals that cause soothing or pleasurable feelings. That stress does not necessarily have to be about body dissatisfaction—people cut for a variety of reasons. However, for people with poor body image, cutting can be a way to express feelings of shame about their body. Some cutters even carve body-shaming words into their flesh as a way of punishing their own bodies.

Actress and musician Demi Lovato struggled with depression, bulimia, and self-harm in her teens. She said that she cut herself "as a way of expressing my own shame, of myself, on my own body. I was matching the inside to the outside. And there were some times where my emotions were just so built up, I didn't know what to do. The only way that I could get instant gratification was through an immediate release on myself."[53]

> " For people with poor body image, cutting can be a way to express feelings of shame about their body. "

Only a small percentage of people who struggle with negative body image will hurt themselves or develop a serious illness. However, low self-esteem—the most common consequence of poor body image—also has serious consequences and can affect every aspect of a teen's life. By understanding how negative feelings about the body can lead to destructive thoughts and behaviors, teens will be better equipped to protect themselves and their friends from potentially deadly disorders.

What Are the Consequences of Negative Body Image?

> **❝**For someone genetically predisposed to an eating disorder, dieting caused by a negative body image could trigger one.**❞**

—Tabitha Farrar, "Body Image of Women," Mirror Mirror: Eating Disorders, 2014. www.mirror-mirror.org.

Farrar suffered from anorexia in her teens and early twenties. Now recovered, she writes about her experiences and educates others about eating disorders.

> **❝**I'm wary of conflating body image and eating disorders, and I don't think that they're nearly as connected as they're made out to be. It's not like she who has the worst body image develops the worst eating disorder.**❞**

—Autumn Whitefield-Madrano, "Beside the Point: Appearance Anxiety in Eating Disorders," *The Beheld* (blog), *New Inquiry*, February 27, 2012. http://thenewinquiry.com.

Whitefield-Madrano, who is recovering from an eating disorder, writes about culture, beauty, and personal appearance.

Bracketed quotes indicate conflicting positions.

* Editor's Note: While the definition of a primary source can be narrowly or broadly defined, for the purposes of Compact Research, a primary source consists of: 1) results of original research presented by an organization or researcher; 2) eyewitness accounts of events, personal experience, or work experience; 3) first-person editorials offering pundits' opinions; 4) government officials presenting political plans and/or policies; 5) representatives of organizations presenting testimony or policy.

Primary Source Quotes

66When we become obsessed with our weight and appearance, not only are we unwell physically; we also settle for lives less vivid and fulfilling.99

—Our Bodies Ourselves, "Building a Better Body Image," February 13, 2012. www.ourbodiesourselves.org.

Our Bodies Ourselves is a nonprofit organization that educates girls and women about reproductive health and sexuality.

66Some people [think that] a perfect body somehow equals a perfect life. . . . This is not at all true. [This] way of thinking . . . can, and does, lead to body hatred and extreme dieting.99

—Melissa Fabello, "Eating Disorders and the Media," YouTube, February 24, 2013. www.youtube.com/watch?v=QtwUZLcohhQ#t=190.

Fabello is an eating-disorder survivor who video blogs about body image and eating disorders.

66[Teens with BDD] might stop going to school because they think that everyone in their class is looking at them and thinking they are ugly.99

—Ben Buchanan, interviewed by 102.7 Triple R Radio, Melbourne, Australia, "Body Dysmorphic Disorder—Psychologist Explains—Ben Buchanan," YouTube, September 8, 2013. www.youtube.com/watch?v=YmuqZDiK3-8.

Buchanan is a neuroscientist and psychologist who heads a body dysmorphic treatment clinic in Melbourne, Australia.

66Teenage boys who think they're too skinny when they are actually a healthy weight are at greater risk of being depressed.99

—American Psychological Association, "Fear of Being Too Skinny May Put Teen Boys at Risk for Depression, Steroid Use," EurekAlert!, January 13, 2014. www.eurekalert.org.

The American Psychological Association is the world's largest professional association of psychologists.

❝Some people [who self-injure] have such hatred for themselves and their bodies that they will carve demeaning names on their bodies as a way to remind themselves of how terrible they are.❞

—Colleen Thompson, "Self Injury," Mirror Mirror: Eating Disorders, 2015. www.mirror-mirror.org.

Thompson founded the website Mirror Mirror: Eating Disorders to help in her recovery from an eating disorder.

❝Just as young women may turn to unhealthy ways of achieving a desired body image, young men may also resort to the use of drugs, excessive exercise and restricted food intake in their quest for an ideal masculine body.❞

—Sex Information and Education Council of Canada, "The Idealized Male Body: The Effect of Media Images on Men and Boys," July/August 2013. http://sexualityandu.ca.

The Sex Information and Education Council of Canada works to educate Canadians about sexual health, including the effects on body image of the sexualization of boys and girls in the media.

❝I realized it wasn't normal that I was consuming huge portions of food whenever I was alone. I crammed so much in, and with such intensity, that I scared myself.❞

—Jen Picicci, "How I Conquered Binge Eating Disorder," Psych Central, March 4, 2015. http://psychcentral.com.

Picicci is an intuitive eating counselor who suffered from binge eating disorder.

What Are the Consequences of Negative Body Image?

- A 2015 survey of **3,000 teens** from London, England, found that half of girls **aged 13 to 14** were on a diet.

- The National Eating Disorders Association estimates that **1 to 5 percent** of the population struggle with binge eating disorder.

- According to the National Association of Anorexia Nervosa and Associated Disorders, almost **50 percent** of people with eating disorders also have depression.

- Anorexia is the third-most common chronic illness among adolescents.

- In 2011, a study published in the journal *Psychology of Sport and Exercise* found that female athletes in sports that partially judge on the athlete's appearance (such as gymnastics, ballet, and figure skating) were at the highest risk of developing eating disorders.

- Although scientists are not sure how many people die from eating disorders, a 2009 study published in the *American Journal of Psychiatry* found that the death rate among anorexia sufferers is **4 percent**, among bulimia sufferers **3.9 percent**, and among EDNOS sufferers **5.2 percent**.

Compulsive Behaviors in Body Dysmorphic Disorder

According to the Body Dysmorphic Disorder (BDD) Program at Rhode Island Hospital, people who suffer from BDD exhibit a variety of compulsive behaviors that can interfere with daily life. The most common behaviors are camouflaging (such as wearing a hoodie or a hairstyle that cover part of their face), scrutinizing a single feature on their face or comparing it to others, and compulsively checking their appearance in the mirror. In a study of 507 people who had BDD, almost 90 percent exhibited one or more of these three compulsive behaviors.

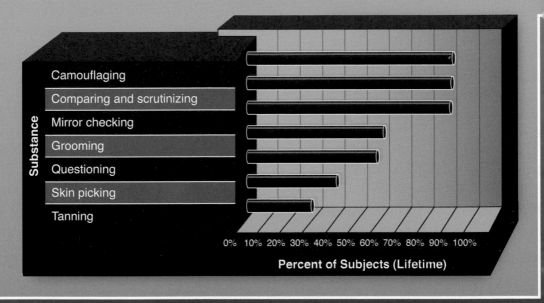

Source: Rhode Island Hospital "Preoccupations and Behaviors," 2014. www.rhodeislandhospital.org.

- According to Purdue University, about **1 million** American males have tried steroids at least once, and up to **6 percent** have taken them before **age 18**.

- According to the National Association of Anorexia Nervosa and Associated Disorders, **95 percent** of people with eating disorders are between **ages 12 and 26**.

Negative Body Image Linked to Unhealthy Weight Control Methods

Psychiatrist Mary Tantillo, the founder of The Healing Connection, an eating-disorder treatment center in New York, examined several large studies about the connection between body dissatisfaction and unhealthy weight control behaviors among teens. In the studies, 57 percent of teen girls and 33 percent of teen boys used unhealthy weight control practices like fasting or skipping meals, and 12 percent of teen girls and 5 percent of teen boys used extreme weight control behaviors like purging or taking diet pills. According to Tantillo, girls who diet are at twelve times the risk of binge eating, and boys are at seven times the risk, compared to girls and boys who do not diet. She concluded that body dissatisfaction predicted extreme weight control behaviors and binge eating and could lead to obesity and eating disorders in vulnerable individuals.

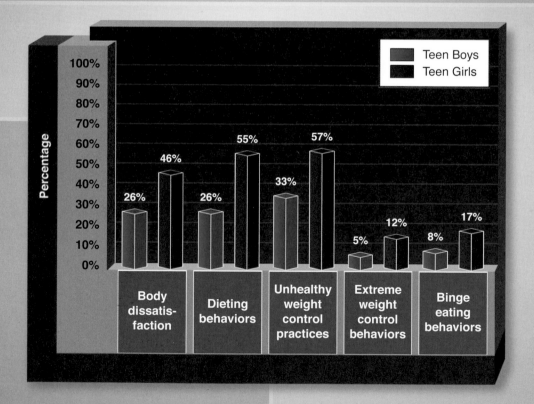

Source: Mary Tantillo, "Special Health Feature: Feeling Good About Our Bodies in Middle School," *Rochester Woman*, May 6, 2012. www.rochesterwomanmag.com.

Symptoms of Major Eating Disorders Are Similar

The three major eating disorders—anorexia nervosa, bulimia nervosa, and binge eating disorder—have similar symptoms and body image disturbances. Even though average body weight varies among the disorders—from underweight in anorexia to overweight in binge eating disorder—people with any of the three disorders are obsessed with weight and appearance. All three groups also experience depression and fatigue.

Eating Disorders Comparison Chart

	Anorexia	Bulimia	Binge Eating Disorder
Weight	Significantly underweight; BMI of less than 17.5	Varies, usually normal weight or overweight	Usually overweight
Eating Habits	Takes in few calories, may eat only a limited variety of foods and may have odd food rituals	Binges by eating large amounts of food in a short period of time, then purges by vomiting and/or abusing laxatives	Binges by eating large amounts of food in a short period of time, may restrict food in between binges
Body Image	Believes she is fat even when she is really underweight; obsessed with weight and appearance	Obsessed with weight and appearance	May be overly focused on weight and appearance
Physical Symptoms	Extreme weight loss, low blood pressure, heart problems, kidney problems, hair loss, lanugo, weakness, fatigue, nutritional deficiencies, cessation of menstruation	Changes in weight, ulcers, sores in the mouth, sore throat, dehydration, dental problems, weakness, fatigue	Excessive weight gain, high blood pressure, diabetes, joint pain, fatigue
Emotional Symptoms	Depression, anxiety, obsessive-compulsive behaviors, denial that there is a problem, fear of gaining weight	Depression, anxiety, feelings of guilt, self-destructive behavior	Depression, feelings of guilt, self-hatred
Relationships	Withdrawn, may refuse to eat in front of others	May be withdrawn but able to develop relationships with others	May be withdrawn, may seem overly sensitive

Source: Duke University, "Eating Disorders in the Classroom," 2014. http://sites.duke.edu.

How Can Teens Improve Their Body Image?

"One day I decided that I was beautiful, and so I carried out my life as if I was a beautiful girl. . . . It doesn't have anything to do with how the world perceives you. What matters is what you see."

—Gabourey Sidibe, an American actor who is noted for her positive body image despite her large size.

"I'm nineteen and I've had enough. No more to [body] comparison and emotional affliction. No more distress caused by preconceived notions of body image. No more to any of it."

—Victoria Erickson, a nineteen-year-old college student who deliberately shared an unflattering picture of herself on social media.

Research has consistently shown that in modern society, looks matter. People who are physically attractive are treated better than those who are not. This creates a dilemma for teenagers who want to feel better about their bodies. How can teens improve their body image in a society that judges them by how they look?

Positive Body Image Is Attractive

Teens who want to change the way they feel about their bodies must remember that having a healthy, positive body image has nothing to do with whether one's body conforms to society's standards of beauty. Teens who have a positive body image ignore society's beauty standards. They feel confident *despite* their appearance.

This confidence can actually make a person appear more physically attractive. A 2009 study in the United Kingdom found that in a group of equally attractive men, those who got a confidence boost from wearing cologne were rated as better looking by women than those who did not. The women watched a fifteen-second video clip of the men and could not smell their cologne. Because the men wearing cologne felt more attractive, they behaved more confidently and therefore were perceived as more attractive.

Focus on What Is Important

One way that teens can improve their body image is to change their focus. People who have healthy body images do not scrutinize their bodies or the bodies of others. They focus on things that matter to them: their friendships, their passions, and their personal growth. Haley Kilpatrick, author of *The Drama Years*, suggests that teens change their focus by getting involved in a nonschool activity. Activities that are physical, like sports or dance, have the added benefit of allowing teens to gain confidence in their bodies. Volunteering is another good way for teens to shift their perspective away from themselves and onto others. "It takes the focus off of the obsessive scrutinizing of each other's looks," Kilpatrick explains. "I know that for me, volunteering at the literacy center was a wakeup call: clients there often didn't have access to dental care and couldn't afford the bare minimum in terms of clothes—and I was obsessing about a potential unibrow?"[54]

Andrew Walen found that he was unable to overcome binge eating disorder until he shifted his focus away from himself and onto the people he loved. "I recovered from my eating disorder by retraining my focus away from body image and self-esteem to the relationships that mattered most to me: my wife, my son, friends, and family,"[55] he explains. After he recovered, Walen founded the Body Image Therapy Center, a treatment center in Columbia, Maryland, that helps people recover from eating disorders,

> "Confidence can actually make a person appear more physically attractive."

substance abuse, self-harm behaviors, and other destructive habits by teaching them to cultivate a positive body image.

Try Therapy or Counseling

Teens who struggle with a disturbed body image—for instance, teens who believe they are bigger or smaller than they actually are—sometimes also suffer from a mental disorder. Teens who struggle with eating disorders, BDD, or depression or self-harm related to body image need the help of a qualified mental health professional to recover. According to the Body Image Therapy Center, "Research shows that talk therapy, especially cognitive therapy (also known as cognitive behavioral therapy), is the most effective way for people to overcome body image disorder."[56] Cognitive behavioral therapy teaches patients to rigorously examine and challenge their thinking patterns and beliefs and to identify errors in thinking about body image—such as believing that a feature on their face is ugly or shocking to others. Patients are encouraged to recognize thoughts that are exaggerated or untrue and to notice how those thoughts affect emotions and behavior.

> A therapist can act as an impartial observer who can put body image issues into perspective.

Therapy is not just effective for teens with disturbed body images, however. All teens who struggle with body image can benefit from therapy or counseling. A therapist can act as an impartial observer who can put body image issues into perspective. Teens can also share their worries and fears with their therapist without having to worry that what they say will be shared with others (licensed therapists are not allowed to discuss what is said in therapy unless someone is in danger). Hayley, a seventh grader, gets help with body image and other issues from her therapist. "She has all of these exercises for calming yourself and focusing your mind, and teaches me not to focus on the bad things,"[57] Hayley says.

Get a Mentor

Kilpatrick also suggests that teens find a mentor—preferably a slightly older teen who has already combated similar body image issues. Mentors can be older siblings or other relatives, members of clubs or teams, or friends who happen to be older. To help teens find mentors, the national organization Girl Talk, founded by Kilpatrick, matches middle school girls with high school girls. Girls interested in starting a local chapter of Girl Talk can learn more at www.mygirltalk.org.

Kilpatrick says that when she was in middle school, her high school mentor, Christie, helped her realize that she was not alone in feeling uncomfortable in her body. It was Kilpatrick's friendship with Christie that inspired her to create Girl Talk. Kilpatrick says:

> I've seen countless girls go from not only surviving but thriving in middle school—thanks to the support and confidence boosters they've received from adopted older sisters. Girls feel comforted by the knowledge that they aren't the only ones who didn't get invited to every sleepover or felt insecure about their looks . . . —and they're hearing it from an older (and therefore cooler!) girl they can emulate and learn from.[58]

Stop Fat Talk and Negative Noise

Experts say that teens who have a healthy social life have a more positive body image. However, friends do not always have a positive influence on body image. Teens who have friends who criticize how others look tend to become more self-conscious about their own appearance.

Similarly, teens who engage in fat talk with their friends tend to have more problems with body image and self-esteem than those who do not. Psychologist Renee Engeln says that fat talk is linked with body shame and eating-disordered behavior. "Fat talk does not motivate women to make healthier choices or take care of their bodies," she explains. "In fact, the feelings of shame it brings about tend to encourage the opposite."[59]

Author Caitlin Boyle engaged in fat talk as a teenager. She calls it "negative noise." In her book *Operation Beautiful*, she writes, "One example of negative noise is telling a friend, 'I feel like a pig in this dress!' when she says she likes

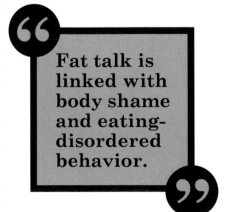

> Fat talk is linked with body shame and eating-disordered behavior.

your outfit. Even if you don't really mean it, negative noise is harmful because it can add up and impact the way you see yourself."[60]

One day when Boyle was struggling with her own inner negative noise, she posted a sticky note on a public bathroom mirror with the words "You are beautiful!" on it. She took a picture of her note and blogged about it, asking others to do the same. Hundreds of people followed her lead and were helped by reading—and writing—the notes, and Boyle posted pictures of the notes on her website, Operation Beautiful. "These little notes make a difference every day," she explains, "healing the scars of bullying, encouraging healthy and balanced living, and promoting a message of inner beauty, not Photoshopped flawlessness."[61] Boyle encourages teens to educate themselves and their friends about the effect fat talk and negative noise have on their body image and self-esteem.

Get Educated

Another way to combat negative body image is to become educated about the way the media—including social media—affects how people feel about their bodies. The US Department of Health and Human Services found that in 2013 adolescents ages eight to eighteen spent an average of seven and a half hours each day using media such as TV and computers (using a computer for school or talking or texting on a mobile phone were not counted in the total). This means that for almost eight hours a day, teens are seeing images of people that have been stylized and digitally edited—including many of the "selfies" of their friends on social media. Such saturation can make it seem as if everyone around them is beautiful.

Learning about how the media manipulates images and perpetuates body image stereotypes can help teens feel better about themselves and their bodies. Online organizations such as the Representation Project help teens educate themselves and each other about these issues. The Representation Project suggests that teens get together to screen the project's 2011 film *Miss Representation* (which examines female stereotypes), or its 2015 film *The Mask You Live In* (which examines male stereotypes).

Some students have organized "no makeup days" at their schools. In 2013 students at Plano Senior High in Texas held a makeup-free Friday to encourage their classmates to feel confident without makeup. "When we first started talking to friends [about the idea], some of them were wary,"[62] said Madeline Milby, one of the event organizers. However, about 80 percent of female students decided to participate. "The atmosphere of school was so lively," said another organizer, student congress president Monica Plenger. "Everyone was in such a good mood and taking pictures. It was a really fun day."[63] Many other schools have held makeup-free days, and the practice of taking makeup-free selfies has become popular online. Dove's Campaign for Real Beauty, a marketing campaign launched in 2004 by the company Unilever, has also promoted makeup-free selfies. The campaign has created various videos, including its 2006 commercial *Dove Evolution* (which can be found on YouTube), which shows the extent to which photographs of models are digitally manipulated.

Does Changing the Body Improve Body Image?

Studies have shown that when people take reasonable action to improve their appearance—such as losing excess weight, getting a haircut, or dressing more attractively—they feel better about themselves and their bodies. However, this boost to self-esteem and body image is often due to being treated differently by one's peers. For example, novelist Lionel Shriver found that her body image improved after her braces came off when she was fifteen. "No longer feeling self-conscious about my front teeth has made me more confident," she explains, "but that just means that being spared all those cracks about Bugs Bunny has helped me to be more completely myself."[64] In her case her body image improved not because her teeth were straight but because she was no longer being teased.

> Invasive cosmetic surgeries . . . are never recommended for teens, in part because their bodies are still changing.

Minor cosmetic surgery that corrects prominent facial features that can attract teasing—such as a large nose or ears—is common among teens and is generally considered by doctors to be safe. However, more-invasive cosmetic surgeries—such as breast augmentation or liposuction—are never recommended for teens, in part because their bodies are still changing. According to Diana Zuckerman, president of the National Center for Health Research, "The average young woman gains weight between the ages of eighteen and twenty-one, and that is likely to change her desire or need for breast augmentation and liposuction."[65] Many teens also find that as they get older, they no longer feel the need to surgically change their bodies. Zuckerman notes that studies show that as teens get older, their body image improves—regardless of whether they have had cosmetic surgery.

> The most effective way for teens to improve their body image is to stop trying to change their bodies and love and accept them as they are.

Despite these warnings, cosmetic surgery is becoming increasingly common among teens. Zuckerman says that more than 236,000 cosmetic procedures were performed on teens in 2012, including more than 75,000 surgical procedures. Before getting cosmetic surgery, teens should fully understand what the surgery entails, including the physical risks and, in the case of breast implants, the need for more surgery later in life to replace aging implants. They also should understand that most people overestimate the psychological benefits of cosmetic surgery and that many people are unhappy with their results. A 2014 survey in the United Kingdom found that 65 percent of people who had plastic surgery said they regretted it, and only 28 percent said that they were happy with the results.

Self-Acceptance Creates Positive Body Image

Though it may seem easier said than done, the most effective way for teens to improve their body image is to stop trying to change their bodies and love and accept them as they are. For instance, Megan Craig was six feet one inch tall when she was twelve years old, and she towered over her classmates. She remembers constantly hunching her shoulders to appear smaller because she was so embarrassed by her height. However, she found that once she embraced the fact that she was tall, others did too. "Some women come up to me and say it's a beautiful thing to be tall, that I should 'work it' and have fun with it. And I do,"[66] she says. Now over six feet eight inches tall, she plays professional basketball for the Washington Wizards.

American actor Gabourey Sidibe, who was nominated for an Academy Award for her portrayal of an obese teenager in the 2009 film

Precious, has also come to terms with her size. "One day I had to sit down with myself and decide that I love myself, no matter what my body looked like and no matter what other people thought of my body,"[67] she said in an interview with Oprah Winfrey. Sidibe and other overweight celebrities, like Lena Dunham, the creator and star of the HBO series *Girls,* see their bodies as a means to express their art. "I think about my body as a tool to do the stuff I need to do," says Dunham, "but not the be all and end all of my existence."[68]

Although it may be challenging for some teens to develop a positive, healthy body image, it is not impossible. Seeking help and support, shifting one's focus, becoming educated about the influence of the media, and striving for self-acceptance are all ways that teens can build confidence in their bodies and in themselves.

Primary Source Quotes*

How Can Teens Improve Their Body Image?

66 People who have low self esteem and go ahead and have [plastic] surgery, long term [they] suffered from more difficult issues, like depression. 99

—Emma Kenny, interviewed by BBC News, "Surgery 'Won't Cure Confidence Issues,'" video, April 24, 2014. www.bbc.com.

Kenny is a registered psychological therapist in the United Kingdom.

66 [Plastic surgery] really changed my life, my happiness, my self-esteem. I felt and feel so much more me and free since my nose-job. 99

—Anja, "How Plastic Surgery Changed My Nose and My Life, Part 2." *Curly Traveller* (blog), March 1, 2014. http://curlytraveller.com.

Anja writes about being bullied about her large nose on her travel blog, *Curly Traveller*.

Bracketed quotes indicate conflicting positions.

* Editor's Note: While the definition of a primary source can be narrowly or broadly defined, for the purposes of Compact Research, a primary source consists of: 1) results of original research presented by an organization or researcher; 2) eyewitness accounts of events, personal experience, or work experience; 3) first-person editorials offering pundits' opinions; 4) government officials presenting political plans and/or policies; 5) representatives of organizations presenting testimony or policy.

❝As teens mature, their body image tends to improve regardless of whether they undergo plastic surgery.❞

—Diana Zuckerman, "Teens and Cosmetic Surgery," Our Bodies Ourselves, May 30, 2014. www.ourbodiesourselves.org.

Zuckerman is an expert on women's health and public policy and is president of the National Center for Health Research.

❝Given that young people today are . . . creating and sharing peer-to-peer media messages about boys' and girls' appearances—they have the tools of change in their hands.❞

—Caroline Knorr, "Is Social Media's 'Camera-Ready' Pressure Bad for Teen Body Image?," *Today*, April 30, 2014. www.today.com.

Knorr is the parenting editor of Common Sense Media, an organization that reviews media for age appropriateness and educational value.

❝I know that the choice to love my body is . . . the key to allowing me to love and respect other people's bodies.❞

—Caroline Rothstein, "Fat Is Not a Feeling," *Thick Dumpling Skin* (blog), February 9, 2015. www.thickdumplingskin.com.

Rothstein is a body empowerment advocate who creates performance art about her struggles with bulimia.

❝People who surround themselves with positive, happy and uplifting friends tend to be more confident and accepting of their own unique body and mind.❞

—Academy of Nutrition and Dietetics, "Body Image and Young Women," EatRight.org, September 23, 2014. www.eatright.org.

The Academy of Nutrition and Dietetics is a professional organization committed to improving the nation's health through research, education, and advocacy.

66Fostering self-compassion—especially among young women who are more overweight—might be another important means by which to increase positive body image and protect against unhealthy weight-control practices.**99**

—Allison C. Kelly et al., "Self-Compassion Moderates the Relationship Between Body Mass Index and Both Eating Disorder Pathology and Body Image Flexibility," *Body Image*, vol. 11, 2014, p. 451.

Kelly is a psychologist and the director of the Self-Attitudes Lab at the University of Waterloo in Ontario, Canada.

66Women will stop worrying about their looks when society stops telling us that they're all we're worth.**99**

—Laura Bates, "Why Is Women's Body Image Anxiety at Such Devastating Levels?," *Guardian* (Manchester, UK), October 14, 2014. www.theguardian.com.

Bates is the founder of the Everyday Sexism Project, a collection of women's daily experiences of gender inequality.

66I could finally ask for cheese fries at a restaurant without spending the rest of the night in a blind panic that everyone thought I was a cow.**99**

—Mandie Williams, "Unpopular Opinion: Pro-Ana Websites Were a Positive Influence in Helping Me Recover from My Eating Disorder," xoJane, April 9, 2014. www.xojane.com.

Williams is a recovered anorexic.

Facts and Illustrations

How Can Teens Improve Their Body Image?

- According to Anorexia Nervosa and Related Eating Disorders, without treatment, up to **20 percent** of people with serious eating disorders die. With treatment, the death rate falls to **2 to 3 percent**.

- Anorexia Nervosa and Related Eating Disorders also states that with treatment, about **60 percent** of people with eating disorders recover, **20 percent** make only partial recoveries, and **20 percent** do not improve.

- According to Diana Zuckerman, president of the National Center for Health Research, in 2012 more than **236,000 cosmetic procedures** were performed on teens, including more than **75,000 surgical procedures**.

- According to the website Our Bodies Ourselves, in 2012, **8,204 teens** underwent breast augmentation surgery. In addition, **1,591 teens** received breast lifts.

- Actor Jamie Lee Curtis was one of the first celebrities to call attention to the way the media manipulates images. In 2002 she posed for an unretouched photograph in her underwear, which was published in *More* magazine beside an airbrushed photo taken after a **3-hour makeover**.

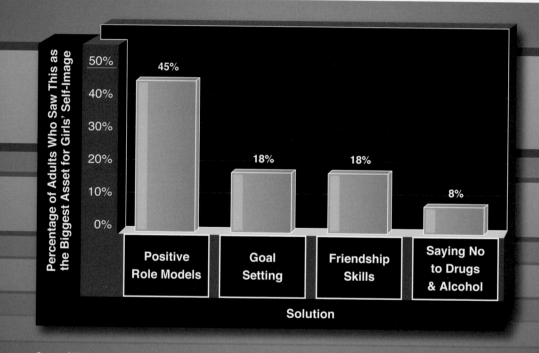

Adults Believe Positive Role Models Help the Most with Body Image

A 2013 survey by GENaustin and Girls Empowerment Network revealed that adults believe that positive role models are the number one solution to teen girls' negative self-image. The survey asked more than two thousand adults in the United States which factors that they thought were most helpful to improving the negative self-image of girls under eighteen years old.

Percentage of Adults Who Saw This as the Biggest Asset for Girls' Self-Image

50%
40%
30%
20%
10%
0%

45%

18%

18%

8%

Positive Role Models

Goal Setting

Friendship Skills

Saying No to Drugs & Alcohol

Solution

Source: GENaustin, "Survey Says: Bullying a Top Concern for Girls' Positive Images, Role Models a Favorite Solution," October 28, 2013. http://genaustin.org.

- In 2006 the fashion industries in Italy and Spain reached voluntary agreements with their governments to ban models from runway shows who did not meet healthy weight criteria, which includes minimum body mass indexes.

- In 2012 the social media sites Tumblr and Pinterest banned material that focuses on self-harming behaviors such as anorexia and bulimia.

Therapy Helps Patients with Body Dysmorphic Disorder

A 2013 metastudy (a study that examines past research) found that most patients with Body Dysmorphic Disorder (BDD) improve after being treated with cognitive behavioral therapy (CBT). Patients who participated in individual and group CBT sessions showed statistically significant decreases in symptoms of BDD and associated depressive symptoms, as measured by diagnostic tests for BDD.

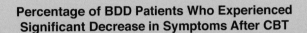

Percentage of BDD Patients Who Experienced Significant Decrease in Symptoms After CBT

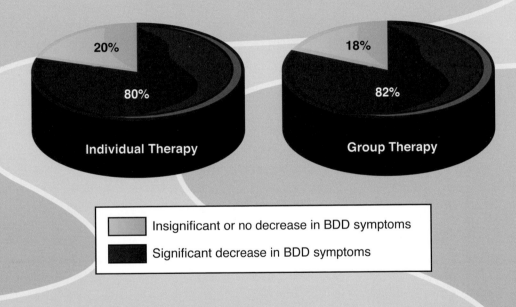

Individual Therapy — 20% / 80%

Group Therapy — 18% / 82%

Insignificant or no decrease in BDD symptoms

Significant decrease in BDD symptoms

Source: Angelica Prazeres et al., "Cognitive-Behavioral Therapy for Body Dysmorphic Disorder: A Review of Its Efficacy," *Journal of Neuropsychiatric Disease and Treatment*, February 28, 2013. www.ncbi.nlm.nih.gov.

- In 2012 *Vogue* magazine announced it would no longer feature teen models who were under **age 16** or models who appeared to suffer from an eating disorder.

- A 2010 national survey by the National Eating Disorders Association found that **85 percent** of American adults believe that insurance companies should cover eating disorders just like any other illness.

Few Young Adults Seek Treatment for Eating Disorders

Most experts estimate that only one in ten people with an eating disorder seeks treatment, with males less likely to seek treatment than females. A 2012 survey of University of Michigan students confirmed this estimate. More than three thousand students participated in U-SHAPE (University Study of Habits, Attitudes and Perceptions around Eating), which was designed to measure multiple aspects of eating and body image. Of those students who screened positive for an eating disorder, 84.3 percent of females and 90.4 percent of males had not sought treatment for their condition. Experts say that the longer one waits to seek treatment for an eating disorder, the greater the chance of relapse.

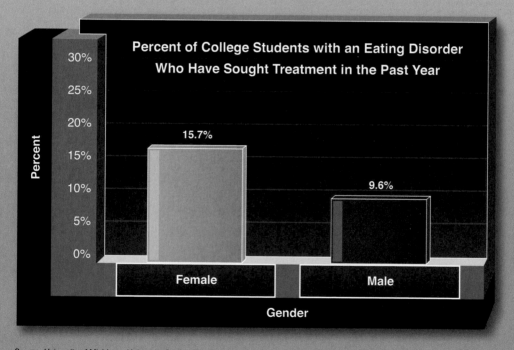

Source: University of Michigan, University Study of Habits, Attitudes, and Perceptions Around Eating, 2013. http://cssl.osu.edu.

- The 2010 survey by the National Eating Disorders Association also found that **70 percent** of adults believe that using more average-sized people in advertising would reduce or prevent eating disorders.

- A survey by the organization Girl Talk found that girls who regularly talked to older girls about issues like body image showed a **14 percent** improvement in math grades and a **24 percent** improvement in language arts grades.

- In 2015 Israel passed a law that required print advertisers to clearly label ads featuring digitally altered images of models.

Key People and Advocacy Groups

007 Breasts: An advocacy group that seeks to improve the body image of girls and women by educating them about the appearance of normal, nonsexualized breasts.

BodyImage3D: A body image advocacy group formed by the Tri Delta fraternity organization, BodyImage3D works to raise body image awareness and education through events, social media initiatives, and its Body Image Ambassadors program.

Caitlin Boyle: The editor of Operation Beautiful, a website dedicated to ending fat talk and fat shaming by encouraging people to post positive messages in public spaces. Boyle speaks and writes about body acceptance and self-esteem.

Geena Davis: An American actor who has worked to promote positive body image and gender diversity in film. Davis is the founder of the Geena Davis Institute on Gender in Media.

Day of the Girl: An advocacy group that raises awareness about the neglect and devaluation of girls around the world and the effect on their body image and self-esteem by promoting the International Day of the Girl (October 11).

Lady Gaga: An American singer and songwriter who struggles with anorexia and bulimia, Gaga launched a project called A Body Revolution 2013 to promote body acceptance. Gaga posted unretouched photographs of herself on the Internet and encouraged others to do the same.

Susie Orbach: A British psychotherapist, Orbach wrote the groundbreaking book *Fat Is a Feminist Issue* in 1978, which explored the relationship between fat, food, and body image. She is a vocal advocate for positive body image among women.

Katharine A. Phillips: A professor of psychiatry at Rhode Island Hospital and director of its Body Dysmorphic Disorder Program, Phillips is widely regarded as one of the leading experts on BDD.

Proud2BMe: An online community of teens and young adults organized by the National Eating Disorders Association. Teens and young adults share stories about their struggles with and triumphs over negative body image and advocate for positive body image among teens.

Cameron Russell: An American fashion model, Russell speaks out about how she benefits from the value that society places on physical appearance. The video of her presentation at the 2012 TEDxMidAtlantic conference became one of TED's most popular talks of all time.

Lizzie Velasquez: A motivational speaker and author, Velasquez suffers from an extremely rare congenital disease that prevents her from retaining body fat. Velasquez weighs 64 pounds (29 kg) and is blind in one eye. Dubbed the "world's ugliest woman" by critics on the Internet, she promotes body acceptance by speaking about her experiences.

Chronology

1984
The Renfrew Center, the first residential facility exclusively dedicated to the treatment of eating disorders, opens in Philadelphia.

1991
Noted feminist Naomi Wolf publishes *The Beauty Myth*, which argues that as women have gained power in society, the expectation that they adhere to standards of physical beauty has grown stronger.

2004
Dove's Campaign for Real Beauty is launched. The marketing campaign features videos that promote natural beauty and positive body image.

1980   1990   2000

1988
Thomas and John Knoll create Photoshop, a pixel-imaging computer program that allows images in digital photographs to be altered.

2003
Actor Kate Winslet publically criticized *GQ* magazine for excessively altering a photograph of her to make her look thin.

2006
Fashion models Luisel Ramos and Ana Carolina Reston die of anorexia, prompting several countries to ban the hiring of fashion models who are dangerously thin.

2015
Unretouched photographs from a 2013 photo shoot of forty-seven-year-old model Cindy Crawford are leaked online. Crawford is praised in the media for her body confidence. Also, American singer-songwriter Meghan Trainor is nominated for a Grammy Award for her song "All About That Bass," which is lauded as being a body-positive anthem for women.

2012
GlobalDemocracy.com releases the video clip *Body Evolution*, a time-lapse video that shows how the bodies of models are digitally altered in photographs. The video clip went viral and has been viewed more than 22 million times.

2010
Isabelle Caro dies from anorexia.

2010

2007
French fashion model Isabelle Caro, who suffered from anorexia, poses nude for a shocking billboard photo for the No.l.ita fashion house's No Anorexia campaign.

2013
Binge eating disorder is officially recognized as an eating disorder in the fifth edition of the *Diagnostic and Statistical Manual for Mental Disorders*, the manual used by doctors to diagnose mental disorders.

2011
Actor and singer-songwriter Demi Lovato publically criticizes the Disney Channel for mocking eating disorders and using increasingly thinner girls on its shows.

2014
Congress introduces the Truth in Advertising Act, which calls for the Federal Trade Commission to study the effect of the use of altered images in advertising.

Related Organizations

Association for Body Image Disordered Eating (ABIDE)
University of California–Davis
1 Shields Ave.
Davis, CA 95616
website: http://abide.ucdavis.edu/resources

ABIDE is dedicated to raising awareness about society's influence on a person's relationship with food and the body. The resources section of its website contains information about eating disorders and negative body image issues, including books, articles, and links to other organizations.

Body Dysmorphic Disorder Program at Rhode Island University
Rhode Island Hospital
Coro Center W., Suite 2.030
1 Hoppin St.
Providence, RI 02903
phone: (401) 444-1644
fax: (401) 444-1645
e-mail: bdd@lifespan.org
website: www.rhodeislandhospital.org/psychiatry/body-image-program.html

The Body Dysmorphic Disorder Program at Rhode Island Hospital is one of the few specialty centers in the country for BDD. Its website contains general information about BDD as well as a list of publications, videos, and other resources.

Centre for Appearance Research
UWE Frenchay
Coldharbour Lane
Bristol
BS16 1QY
United Kingdom
phone: +44 (0) 117 32 82497
e-mail: car@uwe.ac.uk
website: www1.uwe.ac.uk/hls/research/appearanceresearch.aspx

The Centre for Appearance Research at the University of the West of England carries out research in appearance, disfigurement, body image, and related studies. Its website contains information about past and present projects and links to videos and news articles about body image and appearance.

Dove Campaign for Real Beauty

website: www.dove.us/Social-Mission/campaign-for-real-beauty.aspx

A worldwide marketing campaign launched in 2004 by the company Unilever that promotes body acceptance among women through advertisements, video, workshops, and other events. The website contains a collection of videos, articles, statistics, and other resources about body image and body acceptance.

Geena Davis Institute on Gender in Media

Mount Saint Mary's University
12001 Chalon Rd.
Los Angeles, CA 90049
website: www.thegeenadavisinstitute.org

Founded in 2004 by Academy Award–winning actor and advocate Geena Davis, the institute is the only research-based organization working within the media to engage, educate, and influence the need for gender balance, reducing stereotyping, and promoting media literacy. The organization's website contains a wealth of educational and research materials about the effects of gender stereotyping in the media on children and teens.

Girl Talk

3490 Piedmont Rd. NE, Suite 1104
Atlanta, GA 30305
website: www.mygirltalk.org

An international peer-to-peer mentoring program in which high school girls mentor middle school girls about issues related to body image, self-esteem, and bullying. The organization's website has a list of resources about these issues, as well as information about starting a mentoring program.

International OCD Foundation (IOCDF)
PO Box 961029
Boston, MA 02196
phone: (617) 973-5801
fax: (617) 973-5803
e-mail: info@iocdf.org
website: http://bdd.iocdf.org

The IOCDF is an online resource dedicated to providing resources for OCD and related disorders. A section of its website provides information about BDD, including information for professionals, for teens, and for families, as well as information about subtypes of BDD.

National Association of Anorexia Nervosa and Related Disorders (ANAD)
750 E. Diehl Rd., #127
Naperville, IL 60563
phone: (630) 577-1333
e-mail: anadhelp@anad.org
website: www.anad.org

ANAD seeks to prevent and alleviate the problems of anorexia nervosa, bulimia nervosa, and binge eating disorder by promoting education and research. Its website contains general information about eating disorders as well as articles and educational materials about the relationship between body image and eating disorders.

National Center for Overcoming Overeating
website: www.overcomingovereating.com

Launched in 1995, the National Center for Overcoming Overeating is an educational and training organization that works to end body hatred and dieting. The organization's website contains facts, newsletters, and resources about body image and the diet industry, as well as a video workshop series on intuitive eating and overcoming body hatred.

National Eating Disorders Association (NEDA)

165 W. Forty-Sixth St., Suite 402
New York, NY 10036
phone: (212) 575-6200
fax: (212) 575-1650
e-mail: info@nationaleatingdisorders.org
website: www.nationaleatingdisorders.org

The NEDA is an excellent source of information about body image and eating disorders. Its website contains links to research, resources, conferences, and advocacy opportunities, as well as National Eating Disorders Awareness Week, which is organized by NEDA.

Representation Project

PO Box 437
Ross, CA 94957
phone: (415) 386-1200
website: http://therepresentationproject.org

The Representation Project was founded in response to the public reaction to the 2011 film *Miss Representation*, which exposed the way that stereotypes affect the body image of women and girls and limit their participation in society. The organization inspires individuals and communities to overcome gender stereotypes through education and advocacy. The website contains links to videos, statistics, tools, and articles about the ways that stereotypes can affect self-esteem and body image of both boys and girls.

For Further Research

Books

Carrie Arnold, *Decoding Anorexia*. New York: Routledge, 2013.

Thomas Cash and Linda Smolak, eds., *Body Image: A Handbook of Science, Practice, and Prevention*. New York: Guilford, 2012.

Haley Kilpatrick, *The Drama Years*. New York: Simon & Schuster, 2012.

Carol Langlois, *Girl Talk: Boys, Bullies and Body Image*. Madison, VA: Anderson, 2014.

James Lock and Daniel Le Grange, *Help Your Teenager Beat an Eating Disorder*. 2nd ed. New York: Guilford, 2015.

Jane Megan Northrop, *Reflecting on Cosmetic Surgery: Body Image, Shame and Narcissism*. New York: Routledge, 2012.

Victor Strasburger et al., *Children, Adolescents, and the Media*. Thousand Oaks, CA: Sage, 2014.

Julia Taylor, *The Body Image Workbook for Teens*. Oakland, CA: New Harbinger, 2014.

Periodicals

Rhiannon Lucy Cosslett, "'I Feel Guilty but I Hate My Body': A Feminist Confesses," *Guardian* (Manchester, UK), November 8, 2014.

Renee Engeln, "The Problem with 'Fat Talk,'" *New York Times*, March 13, 2015.

Olivia Fleming, "'Why Don't I Look Like Her?': How Instagram Is Ruining Our Self Esteem," *Elle*, November 18, 2014.

Sarah Gervais, "Does Instagram Promote Positive Body Image?," *Psychology Today*, January 22, 2013.

Carrie Gottlieb, "Disordered Eating or Eating Disorder: What's the Difference?," *Psychology Today*, February 23, 2014.

Ruth Graham, "Who Will Fight the Beauty Bias?," *Boston Globe*, August 23, 2013.

Jamie Santa Cruz, "Body-Image Pressure Increasingly Affects Boys," *Atlantic*, March 10, 2014.

Lionel Shriver, "Warning: I Will Employ the Word 'Fat,'" *New York*, August 19, 2013.

Internet Sources

Cleveland Clinic Foundation, "Fostering a Positive Self-Image," Cleveland Clinic, November 4, 2013. http://my.clevelandclinic.org/health /healthy_living/hic_Stress_Management_and_Emotional_Health /hic_Fostering_a_Positive_Self-Image.

Caroline Knorr, "Is Social Media's 'Camera-Ready' Pressure Bad for Teen Body Image?," *Today*, April 30, 2014. www.today.com/style/social -medias-camera-ready-pressure-bad-teen-body-image-2D79601219.

Carleigh O'Connell, "Putting the Words 'Behind' Me: A 14-Year-Old Mighty Girl Takes a Stand Against Body Shaming," *A Mighty Girl* (blog), July 23, 2014. www.amightygirl.com/blog?p=7083.

Samantha Olson, "Body Image Issues in Middle School Teens Worsen in Presence of Older Girls," Medical Daily, September 18, 2014. www .medicaldaily.com/body-image-issues-middle-school-teens-worsen -presence-older-girls-303876.

Carolyn Ross, "Why Do Women Hate Their Bodies?," Psych Central, June 2, 2012. http://psychcentral.com/blog/archives/2012/06/02 /why-do-women-hate-their-bodies.

Emily Sohn, "Why We Don't See Ourselves as Others Do," Discovery News, April 24, 2013. http://news.discovery.com/human/psychol ogy/why-we-dont-see-ourselves-as-others-do-130423.htm.

Kavita Varma-White, "Body Image Isn't Just a 'Girl Thing': Boys Suffer Too," *Today*, April 30, 2014. www.today.com/style/body-image -isnt-just-girl-thing-boys-suffer-too-2D79592420.

Jill Weber, "4 Ways Social Media Can Undermine Girls and Women," *Huffington Post*, November 17, 2014. www.huffingtonpost.com/jill -p-weber-phd-/four-ways-social-media-ca_b_5830540.html.

Autumn Whitefield-Madrano, "The Mainstream Myth About Eating Disorders," *Salon*, February 27, 2012. www.salon.com/2012/02/27 /eating_disorders_open2012.

Source Notes

Overview

1. Haley Kilpatrick, *The Drama Years: Real Girls Talk About Surviving Middle School*. New York: Free Press, 2012. Kindle edition.
2. Quoted in Emily Sohn, "Why We Don't See Ourselves as Others Do," Discovery News, April 24, 2013. http://news.discovery.com.
3. Cleveland Clinic, "Fostering a Positive Self-Image," November 4, 2013. http://my.clevelandclinic.org.
4. Brown University, "Body Image." www.brown.edu.
5. Brown University, "Body Image."
6. Rebecca Puhl, "Child Obesity and Stigma," Obesity Action Coalition, 2015. www.obesityaction.org.
7. Quoted in Ruth Graham, "Who Will Fight the Beauty Bias?," *Boston Globe*, August 23, 2013. www.bostonglobe.com.
8. Lisa Damour, "Video Series: Teenagers and Body Image," *Your Teen*, 2014. http://yourteenmag.com.
9. Kilpatrick, *The Drama Years*.
10. Quoted in Kilpatrick, *The Drama Years*.
11. Kilpatrick, *The Drama Years*.
12. Cleveland Clinic, "Fostering a Positive Self-Image."
13. Carleigh O'Connell, "Putting the Words 'Behind' Me: A 14-Year-Old Mighty Girl Takes a Stand Against Body Shaming," *A Mighty Girl* (blog), July 23, 2014. www.amightygirl.com.

What Issues Do Teens Have with Their Bodies?

14. Quoted in Kilpatrick, *The Drama Years*.
15. Eleanor Wertheim and Susan Paxton, "Body Image Development in Adolescent Girls," in *Body Image: A Handbook of Science, Practice, and Prevention*, edited by Thomas Cash and Linda Smolak. New York: Guilford, 2012, p. 77.
16. Quoted in Kavita Varma-White, "Body Image Isn't Just a 'Girl Thing': Boys Suffer Too," *Today*, April 30, 2014. www.today.com.
17. Kimberly Couzens, "How I Learned to Love Being Tall," *The Blog, Huffington Post*, July 12, 2012. www.huffingtonpost.com.
18. Quoted in Bess Manson, "Life as a Short Man: The Psychology of Height," Stuff, April 10, 2014. www.stuff.co.nz.
19. Quoted in Varma-White, "Body Image Isn't Just a 'Girl Thing.'"
20. Quoted in American Psychological Association, "Fear of Being Too Skinny May Put Teen Boys at Risk for Depression, Steroid Use," January 13, 2014. www.apa.org.
21. Michael Gartner, "How Common Is Breast Asymmetry Among Women?," RealSelf, November 11, 2014. www.realself.com.
22. CNN Wire, "Is Your Penis Size 'Normal'? New Research Exposes How You Measure Up," CBS 6, March 6, 2015. http://wtvr.com.
23. Quoted in Rachel Zar, "Labiaplasty: What's a 'Normal' Vagina?," Refinery29, October 15, 2013. www.refinery29.com.
24. SexInfo Online, "Labiaplasty," February 2, 2012. www.soc.ucsb.edu.

What Contributes to Negative Body Image?

25. Caroline Knorr, "Is Social Media's 'Camera-Ready' Pressure Bad for Teen Body Image?," *Today*, April 30, 2014. www.today.com.
26. Carolyn Ross, "Why Do Women Hate Their Bodies?," *World of Psychology* (blog), Psych Central, June 2, 2012. http://psychcentral.com.
27. Kilpatrick, *The Drama Years*.
28. Jean Kilbourne, "Women's Bodies in Advertising," Our Bodies Ourselves, February 13, 2012. www.ourbodiesourselves.org.
29. Quoted in Sex Information and Education Council of Canada, "The Idealized Male Body: The Effect of Media Images on Men and Boys," July/August 2013. http://sexuality andu.ca.
30. Sex Information and Education Council of Canada, "The Idealized Male Body."
31. Tiffany, "The (Lack of) Breasts in Media," *The Feminist Fist* (blog), July 17, 2013. https://feministfist.wordpress.com.
32. Kelly R., "My Breasts Almost Ruined My Life," *Cosmopolitan*, April 10, 2014. www .cosmopolitan.com.
33. Puhl, "Child Obesity and Stigma."
34. Puhl, "Child Obesity and Stigma."
35. Quoted in Jennifer Pastiloff, "The Love Campaign," *The Manifest-Station* (blog), November 23, 2013. http://themanifeststation.net.
36. Marika Tiggemann, "Sociocultural Perspectives on Human Appearance and Body Image," in *Body Image: A Handbook of Science, Practice, and Prevention*, edited by Thomas Cash and Linda Smolak. New York: Guilford, 2012, p. 16.
37. Jill Weber, "4 Ways Social Media Can Undermine Girls and Women," *Huffington Post*, November 17, 2014. www.huffingtonpost.com.
38. Sarah Gervais, "Does Instagram Promote Positive Body Image?," *Power and Prejudice* (blog), *Psychology Today*, January 22, 2013. www.psychologytoday.com.

What Are the Consequences of Negative Body Image?

39. Quoted in Kilpatrick, *The Drama Years*.
40. Quoted in Kilpatrick, *The Drama Years*.
41. Quoted in Kilpatrick, *The Drama Years*.
42. Carrie Gottlieb, "Disordered Eating or Eating Disorder: What's the Difference?," *Psychology Today*, February 23, 2014. www.psychologytoday.com.
43. Quoted in Youth Health Talk, "Myths About Eating Disorders," 2014. www.healthtalk .org.
44. Gottlieb, "Disordered Eating or Eating Disorder."
45. Josie Tuttle, "The Thin Line Between Diet and Eating Disorder," GoodTherapy.org, August 26, 2011. www.goodtherapy.org.
46. Linda Smolak and J. Kevin Thompson, eds., *Body Image, Eating Disorders, and Obesity in Youth*. Washington, DC: American Psychological Association, 2013. Kindle edition.
47. Katharine Phillips, interviewed by Kevin Wandler, "Body Dysmorphic Disorder," University of Florida Department of Psychiatry, February 10, 2012. www.youtube.com /watch?v=t1qlVCvARNE.
48. Phillips, interview.
49. Ben Buchanan, interviewed by 102.7 Triple R Radio, Melbourne, Australia, "Body Dysmorphic Disorder," September 8, 2013. www.youtube.com/watch?v=YmuqZDiK3-8.

50. Body Dysmorphic Disorder Program, "Body Dysmorphic Disorder in Children and Adolescents," Rhode Island Hospital, 2014. www.rhodeislandhospital.org.

51. Robert Olivardia et al., "Muscle Dysmorphia," International OCD Foundation, 2015. http://bdd.iocdf.org.

52. Quoted in Jamie Santa Cruz, "Body-Image Pressure Increasingly Affects Boys," *Atlantic*, March 10, 2014. www.theatlantic.com.

53. Quoted in Kilpatrick, *The Drama Years*.

How Can Teens Improve Their Body Image?

54. Kilpatrick, *The Drama Years*.

55. Andrew Walen, "What's Your Passion?," Body Image Therapy Center, February 8, 2015. http://thebodyimagecenter.com.

56. Body Image Therapy Center, "Body Image and Self Esteem." http://thebodyimagecenter.com.

57. Quoted in Kilpatrick, *The Drama Years*.

58. Kilpatrick, *The Drama Years*.

59. Renee Engeln, "The Problem with 'Fat Talk,'" *New York Times*, March 13, 2015. www.nytimes.com.

60. Caitlin Boyle, *Operation Beautiful: One Note at a Time*. New York: Penguin, 2012. Kindle edition.

61. Boyle, *Operation Beautiful*.

62. Quoted in Danika Fears, "Students Go Without Makeup for a Day at Texas High School," *Today*, March 11, 2013. www.today.com.

63. Quoted in Fears, "Students Go Without Makeup for a Day at Texas High School."

64. Lionel Shriver, "Warning: I Will Employ the Word 'Fat,'" *New York*, August 19, 2013. http://nymag.com.

65. Diana Zuckerman, "Teens and Cosmetic Surgery," Our Bodies Ourselves, May 30, 2014. www.ourbodiesourselves.org.

66. Quoted in Manson, "Life as a Short Man."

67. Quoted in Corinne Heller, "OTRC: Gabourey Sidibe Has Best Response to Critics over Her Golden Globes Look," ABC7 Eyewitness News, January 12, 2014. http://abc7.com.

68. Quoted in Jen Carlson, "Lena Dunham Tells Us About Her 'Zen Body Philosophy,'" *The Gothamist* (blog), January 16, 2014. http://gothamist.com.

List of Illustrations

Index